What do Online Safety Experts and Moms Have to Say About Facebook Guide for Parents?

What Parents Need to Know About Facebook

Written by Safe Family Online

As an **Internet Safety Advocate**, for CyberSafeFamily.com, I speak locally to schools, PTA meetings, youth groups, churches and community events. Every time I speak to tweens/teens and parents, I discuss Facebook and how it can impact our **online reputation**.

This is an excellent tool for me and I believe, **a "must have" for any parent that has a teen on Facebook.**

. . . .

Facebook Guide for Parents - Today's Internet Safety Must-Have Reference

Written by Janis Brett Elspas, MommyBlogExpert

In case you're wondering, the reason why I feel so strongly about this new book it's because I am a concerned and very involved parent of four kids: triplets who are almost 13, and big brother 14. I am also Internet safety for children advocate and a Certified Online Mom in The Online Mom Network Facebook and other social networks such as MySpace and Twitter are very much a part of your kids' and my kids' lives today.

Facebook Guide for Parents is an essential parenting reference guide for the fast-paced cyber world we live in, a book that no household with any kids ages 3 - 18 who should be without. If my own experience with this

© SupremeSocialMedia.com

FREMONT PUBLIC LIBRARY DISTRICT
1170 N. Midlothian Road
Mundelein, IL 60060

publication so far is any indication – it is one that you will constantly be referring back to again and again.

· ·

The Facebook Guide Every Parent MUST Read!

*Written by Kim Cantrell,
Founder of The Mom Trap*

This easy-to-understand and use guide tells parents everything they need to know about establishing their own presence on Facebook and monitoring their children's accounts. A no-muss, no-fuss guide that gets straight to the point. No fluff. No filler. Everything you need to know to get started on Facebook in under half an hour.

· ·

Sandy Kalosky, Retired Middle School Teacher

I was quite impressed with the depth of the explanations. Based on the impulsivity factor that is firmly embedded in most adolescent minds, I think this presentation would be extremely valuable for schools to incorporate into their personal safety/Guidance or Computer classes. The very user-friendly presentation format was not overwhelming to me (a non-facebook user presently); furthermore, as I was guided through the areas regarding 'privacy settings' and 'appropriate comments' (to name just a couple), I was impressed with the information, the gentle warnings, and the demonstrations. The suggested warnings for parents to consider sharing with their children was extremely relevant.

Finally, I must tell you that if I had an adolescent in my home who was either on 'Facebook' or considering it, your product would be read by both of us - not just to give us something to talk about, but to reinforce the fact that as a parent, my 'job' is to protect and prepare my child for our technological world to the best of my ability. Thank you so much for

© SupremeSocialMedia.com

sharing this very unique product. Well done.

• • • • • • • • • • • • • • • • • • • •

Facebook Guide for Parents - Safeguard your Teens
Written by Jennifer Wagner,
Founder, Connect with Your Teens

If you are like many parents lately, there is a fairly good chance you have already joined Facebook. Your teens or tweens may or may not have friended you on it, but you feel confident that you know what you should about this social networking site that your child spends so much time on. I know that I thought I did. Was I surprised to see how much I didn't know about how Facebook works when I read The Facebook Guide for Parents

• • • • • • • • • • • • • • • • • • • •

Facebook Guide For Parents
Written by Linda Heuer
Founder, www.MomTechnology.com

Facebook guide for parents is wonderful! Simple, quick, easy, what more can us busy Moms ask for?

If you have a child who is thinking about setting up a Facebook account and you are not sure they are ready, Facebook guide will help. The pages are full of helpful tips through which you will be able to make an informed decision. If you and your child do decide it is time for a Facebook account then your child can sign the contract Facebook guide has provided. Oh yeah, a contract! These ladies know what they are doing.

• • • • • • • • • • • • • • • • • • • •

"Wow, these tutorials are fantastic! Extremely professional and well done. I think this is a wonderful tool for parents and I can't wait to share it with my subscribers."

© SupremeSocialMedia.com

Rhonda Ryder,
Founder, www.KidsAwakening.com
and www.HappierKidsNow.com

• • • • • • • • • • • • • • • • • • •

"I just love it when I find a clear, concise guide that caters to different learning styles. Facebook Guide for Parents presents a written guide, that seems to go just at the right pace for me to take in this vital information, to help me protect my child online."

Annie Oliveri, Festival Director, HappyKidsFestival.com

• • • • • • • • • • • • • • • • • • •

"This must read guide helps parents understand the power of Facebook in their children's lives. By educating themselves, parents learn their teen's language along with learning how to keep them safe. Pay particular attention to the Groups section. Knowing the Groups your teen joins, gives insight into their thoughts and feelings and is a great springboard for initiating powerful conversations. We must stay connected to have influence. This guide is the tool you need to connect through Facebook."

Sandra Dye, Child & Parenting Expert
www.One-Step-Ahead-Parenting.com

• • • • • • • • • • • • • • • • • • •

To the wonderful people at Supreme Social Media,

"I want to thank you for your valuable product Facebook for Parents. It's about time someone put together a program like this. Many of us parents are just learning the ropes ourselves and although I thought I was pretty Facebook savvy, I will admit while reading through the booklet, I took numerous notes of things I needed to go and check in my own personal Facebook page settings and wow…I had more than a few changes to make.

 © SupremeSocialMedia.com

There were things I just really wasn't aware of or as educated on as I should have been. Furthermore I love the section you provide on Cyber bullying, as this too is something I hadn't given much thought to. It's an ever changing world and I'm sure I'm not the first parent who has commented about wishing there was a parenting manual. Thanks to you and Supreme Social Media at least there now is a manual for parenting children on Facebook of which I will highly recommend to my friends.

After having read through the program, I sat my son down and he and I went through all of his settings while I explained to him the pro's and con's of each step. Unfortunately I don't think our children realize the implications these sites can have in the future as far as college applications, job searches etc.

The Facebook for Parents Guide is a must read! Thank you once again for helping to make parenting a bit easier and Facebook a lot more safe and fun!"

Sincerely,
Gina McNew, Entrepreneur and Founder of www.ItsHiptoBeHot.com

• •

"Facebook for Parents is powerful! Step by step, easy to follow instructions on how to protect our children and monitor their activities and who they are associating with. Once again, the Supreme Social Girls have added more value to keeping us safe in Cyber World. Their videos and guide books go hand in hand. Thank you girls for all you do."

Lyn-Dee Eldridge, CPC, CPMC
www.Lyn-Dee.com

• •

"Incredible! The presentation is clear, concise and informative. I recommend these tools for any parent starting out on Facebook!"

Tamara Monosoff, Founder & CEO of Mom Inventors, Inc.
www.MomInvented.com

"I was thrilled with the utter amount of information provided in The Facebook Guide For Parents! Even as a member of Facebook for about 2 years, I learned about privacy settings, blocking people, search options and much more that I wasn't aware of before. When my younger daughter is old enough to become a member, I will make use of the tools provided. "

www.BrainFoggles.com

Introduction

Today we live in a world where technological advances seem to happen at the speed of light, with our children leading the charge.

This book is dedicated to all the parents who remember a world where:

- **TV had only 3 channels and a dial that you had to get up and change**
- **we used typewriters for school papers and whiteout if we made mistakes**
- **the biggest advance in photography was the Polaroid picture**
- **we used the phone book to find telephone numbers**
- **the only way to send a message to someone was through the post office, with a stamp**
- **we were taught DOS in computer class**
- **Atari asteroids, pong and Super Mario Brothers were our video games**
- **we needed a dime and a payphone to call our parents if we were going to be late on a Saturday night**
- **we called our iPod a "walkman"**

© SupremeSocialMedia.com

> **There was no internet and NO FACEBOOK**

With all of the emerging technologies in today's landscape, there certainly is the potential for confusion, distraction or misunderstanding. But, there are also new opportunities for communication and connectivity. For example, mobile phones enable us to quickly connect with our loved ones anywhere, anytime. No more need for dimes, or a dimly lit gas-station payphone. We can video conference with someone on a laptop from a coffee shop with wireless access half way across the globe or send email from an airplane, or exchange digital photos within seconds. The opportunities are endless.

As parents, we just need to make sure we understand the types of communication technologies our kids are using so that we can help ensure they use them as safely as possible. The more we know about these very public touch points available to our children, the more we can help them make the right decisions, have fun and stay safe.

Disclaimer: Facebook® Guide for Parents is NOT associated with Facebook® Corporation in any way.

International Copyright laws protect the material contained in this publication. You may not reproduce or resell the content in any manner. The information in this publication is for informational purposes only and in no way is this to be considered legal advice. Facebook® Guide for Parents is not affiliated with Facebook® Corporation in ANY way.
Copyright © 2010. All Rights Reserved.

© SupremeSocialMedia.com

Table of Contents

Preface: Sex, Drugs…Now Facebook? 13

Chapter 1: Signing Up for Facebook 17

Chapter 2: Finishing Up Your Profile 23

Chapter 3: Account Settings 32

    The Networks Tab: 34

    Mobile Tab: 36

    Language Tab: 37

    Payment Tab: 37

    Facebook Ads Tab 37

Chapter 4: Privacy Settings Profile Information 38

    Bio or favorite quotation: 45

    Edit Photo Album Privacy 46

    Relationships: 47

    Photos and Videos I'm tagged in 49

Chapter 5: Privacy Settings - Contact Information 53

Chapter 6: Privacy Settings - Basic Directory Information 55

© SupremeSocialMedia.com

Facebook Internal Search 56

Friend Requests and Private Messages 57

Friends: 58

Chapter 7: Privacy Settings - Applications and Websites 60

The "Instant Personalization" setting 65

Public Search Listing: 68

Privacy settings and joining groups or fan or community pages: 70

Chapter 8: Privacy Settings – Block List and Bullying 71

Chapter 9: The Wall and News Feed 76

Who's that writing on my WALL? 78

Wall and News Feed: Privacy Setting 81

Chapter 10: Finding People on Facebook 83

Chapter 11: Creating Friend List 89

Chapter 12: To Friend or Not to Friend, ... 95

That is the Question 95

Un-friending people: 97

Chapter 13: Friends Options Review 99

Facebook® Guide for Parents 11

© SupremeSocialMedia.com

Chapter 14: Creating User Name Link 102

Chapter 15: Removing Posts 103

Chapter 16: Reputation Monitoring 104

Chapter 17: HELP- My Ungrateful Child "Unfriended" Me! 108

Chapter 18: Joining and Starting Groups 116

    Creating a group on Facebook 117

Chapter 19: Uploading Photos and Videos 122

    Tagging Photos of People: 127
    Sharing Your Photos: 129
    Un-tagging Yourself from Photos/Videos: 131

Chapter 20: Playing Games on Facebook 132

Final Words 136

Supreme Facebook Contract 137

Family Facebook Users Contract 138

Other products by Supreme Social Media 139

Preface: Sex, Drugs...Now Facebook?

Yes, it's true. Now there is ONE MORE thing we as parents have to have "the talk" about. Technology has brought many wonderful things into our lives. We have monitors that let us watch our babies while they sleep. We can TIVO our kid's favorite shows while they are studying. We are only a phone or a text message away at any time. However, with all the great things technology has offered us, it has also introduced some potential downsides as well.

We want to mention here that we LOVE Facebook. Our company - Supreme Social Media - launched to teach business professionals how to engage and use social media platforms, such as Facebook, to enhance and build a client base and online reputation. In addition, we have all used Facebook to connect to long lost friends, relatives and engage in conversations with other people outside our normal sphere of influence.

In our research on the business aspects of connecting, we realized how many people, especially children, are not aware that their **personal** information is posted in cyber-space for all to see. It is for this reason we created this "Facebook Guide for Parents."

All of us involved with Supreme Social Media are moms, aunts and/or sisters. We understand how important it is for parents and guardians to understand these new social networks and all their positive traits, while at the same time protecting you and the young people in your lives from the potential harm they can cause. And we're not just talking about on-line predators. We're talking about their future reputations, college applications and even job interviews that can be affected inadvertently from a long forgotten post on Facebook.

We are not child psychologists, doctors or teachers. But as parents, aunts and sisters, and social media professionals, we have some experience talking to the kids in our lives about safety online and we want to help others do the same. With the information provided here, we encourage you to engage in conversation with your children. We all remember far too clearly the fun and laughter we experienced in our youth, and are secretly glad this type of technology wasn't around to tempt us into making questionable decisions that we might regret today. Polaroid pictures were scary enough. Those

© SupremeSocialMedia.com

pictures of bad hair, college parties and spring break probably would not have been a good thing to have floating around out there on the web then, or today. We have the gift of hindsight, and as parents, it's now our job to point our kids in the right direction online.

Consider these Facebook Statistics (most from Facebook others are sourced as noted):

- **Facebook has 500 million users**
- **If Facebook were a country, it would be the 3rd largest in the world**
- **Over 9 million U.S. children between the ages of 13 and 17 are registered Facebook users.** (source http://www.checkfacebook.com)
- **50% of our active users log on to Facebook in any given day**
- **Average user has 130 friends**
- **People spend over 500 billion minutes per month on Facebook**

Activity on Facebook

- There are over 160 million objects that people interact with (pages, groups and events)
- Average user is connected to 60 pages, groups and events
- Average user creates 70 pieces of content each month
- More than 25 billion pieces of content (web links, news stories, blog posts, notes, photo albums, etc.) shared each month.

Global Reach

- More than 70 translations available on the site
- About 70% of Facebook users are outside the United States

Facebook® Guide for Parents 16

Chapter 1: Signing Up for Facebook

If you don't have a Facebook profile yet, please take the time to read this chapter and to set one up. Chances are your child does have a profile and the only way to find out is if 1) they tell you, 2) you "Google" or search the search engines for their name and their profile comes up or 3) if you have a Facebook profile and can find them yourself. Facebook is a gigantic playground and just as you'd want to get the lay of the land at any physical playground where your child spends time, it's important for you to understand this virtual playground. You'll want to educate your child about safety and you'll want to meet the other adults and children who hang out there.

If you know that your child has a profile, why not ask them to walk you through the set up? You can learn the steps here, but sitting with them makes them more involved in the process and they will take pride in teaching you something. They'll also know that you will now be on Facebook and even this knowledge could help them make better choices when posting comments and interacting with their friends. Telling them you are joining could open up an important dialogue

and, once you've finished reviewing this book, you might even be able to teach them a thing or two!

So, let's get started with setting up a profile:

(even if you've already signed up you may benefit from some of this information, so don't be too quick to jump ahead)

Go to http://facebook.com,

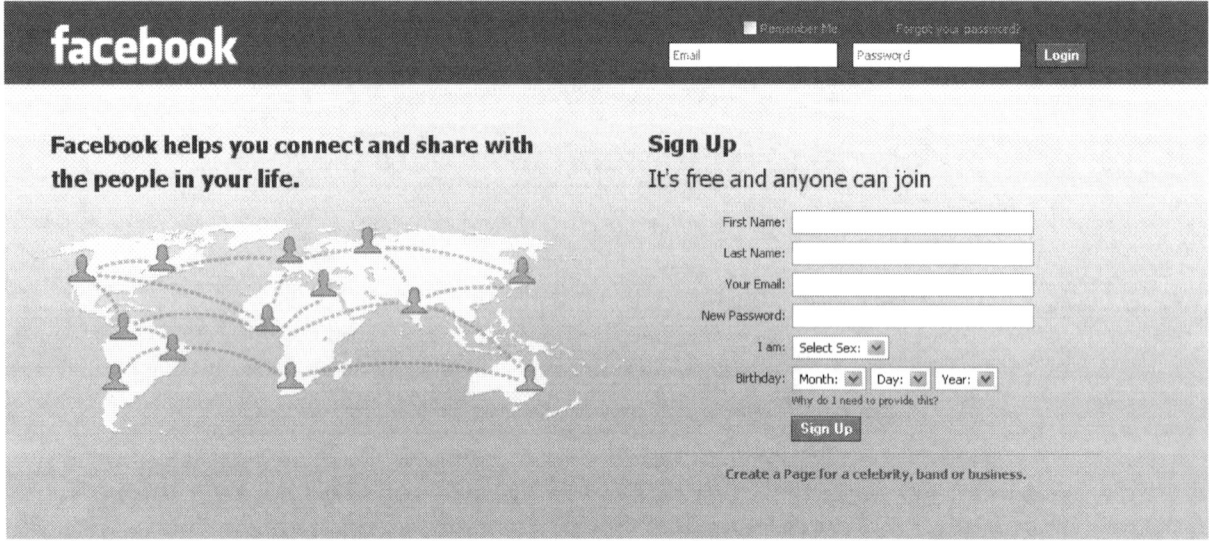

Go ahead and enter your information. Creating an account is free (really). We will show you, step-by-step, how to keep your profile as private as you would like.

Many people ask, "Why do I need to put in my birthday?"

Facebook has a policy that no one under 13 years of age can have an account. That doesn't mean, however that your pre-teen hasn't embellished their birth date to get around this. Facebook works on the honor system and, as we've found out personally, some of our children as young as eleven had active Facebook accounts.

Step 1: Find Friends

We never recommend you give up your email list—ever. But, if you would like to start connecting quickly with friends, go ahead and give your email address and password to allow Facebook to access the email addresses of your friends to match them to their Facebook profiles. Otherwise, just click "skip this step." You can always go back and invite friends later.

Step 2: Profile Information

On this page, you will be asked about your school information. You are not required to complete this section. However, Facebook uses this information to suggest friends for you. It is up to you if you want to provide this information. Even if you provide the information here, you do not need to make it viewable to everyone. You can decide about that later when you establish your privacy settings. If you decide that you do not want to provide this information now, you can always add it later, so click "skip."

Step 3: Profile Picture

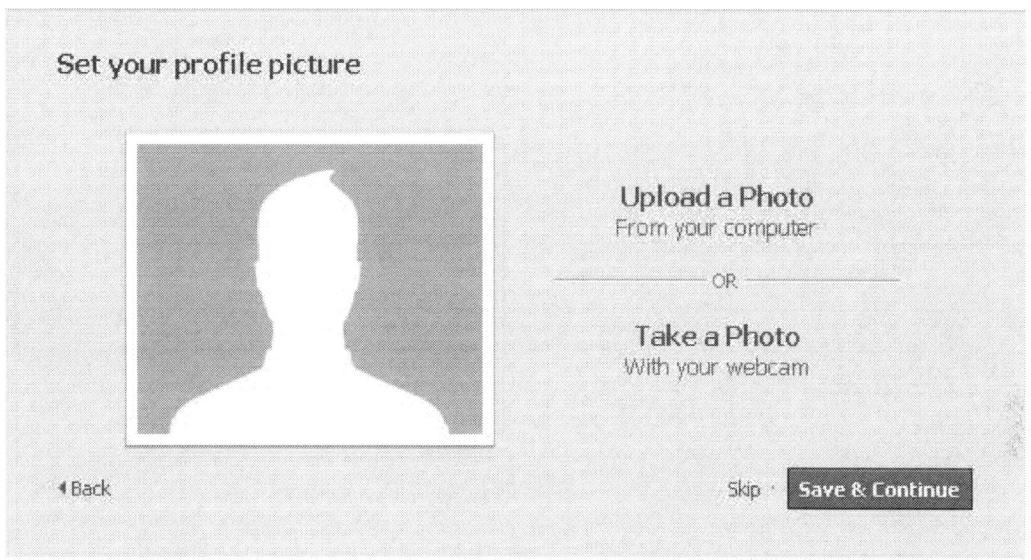

We strongly suggest you upload a photo of yourself here. After all, it is called "face" book. Don't be nervous. You can do this. If you have been using a digital camera and have been storing your photos on your computer or even on a photo-sharing site, this will be simple. Just click on "Upload a photo, then click "Browse" and select a photo of yourself from your computer. Click "upload." Note: This may be one of those tasks you can ask your child to help you with if this is the first time you are doing something like this. However, his or her idea of a "good" photo and yours might be quite different. (Skip the one of you with the crazy glasses.)

© SupremeSocialMedia.com

Last step: Facebook will ask you if you want to find people you know or view and edit your profile. We will go through setting up your whole profile and searching for people in the next few chapters.

Chapter 2: Finishing Up Your Profile

We recommend that you complete your profile set up and then move on to creating your privacy settings because there you'll see the types of information Facebook can capture. **Entering your information in these fields is completely voluntary.** You do not need to answer *any* of the questions in this section or fill out any information. You may include some, all or none of the information Facebook asks you to provide here.

On your blue navigation bar at the top of your page, click "Profile" and you will come to your profile page.

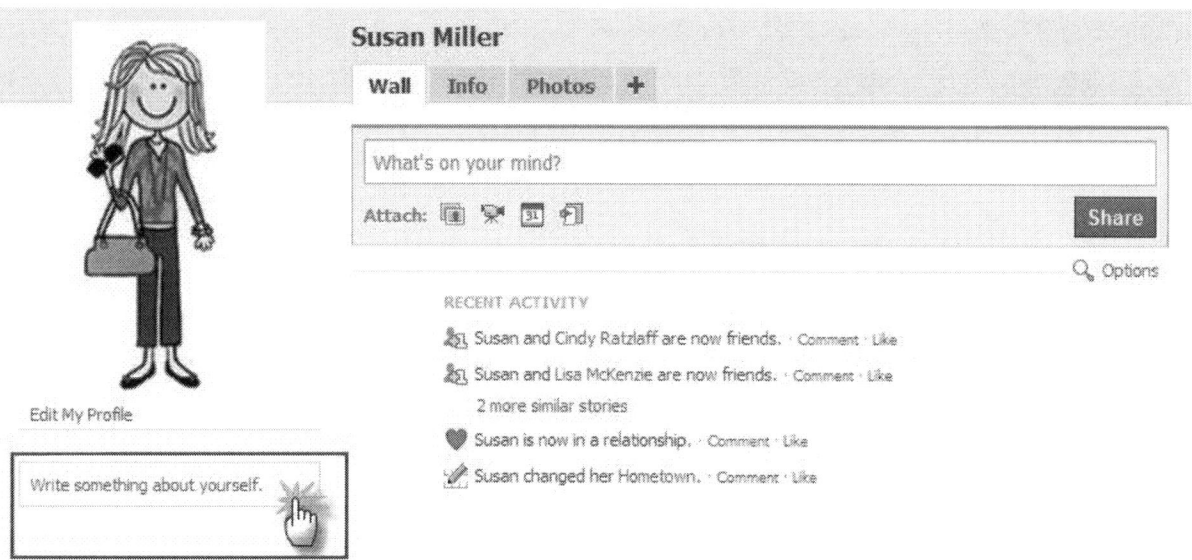

One of the first things you can do is click on "Write something about yourself." Here you can put a short paragraph that

Facebook® Guide for Parents 23

© SupremeSocialMedia.com

describes you and helps people who visit your profile identify who you are. Here are some examples:

> Wife, mother, entrepreneur and passionate speaker on web and social media marketing. Love to laugh and take long walks on the beach. Great to connect with you here!

> Certified Social Media Strategist with a passion for books and people who write them. Award winning marketing and publicity executive with 20+ years experience in creating best sellers and buzz worth messages. Former improv comedian.

Add more information to your personal profile. To edit your profile click "Edit My Profile" below your picture. Once you do that, you will be taken to this Basic Information screen:

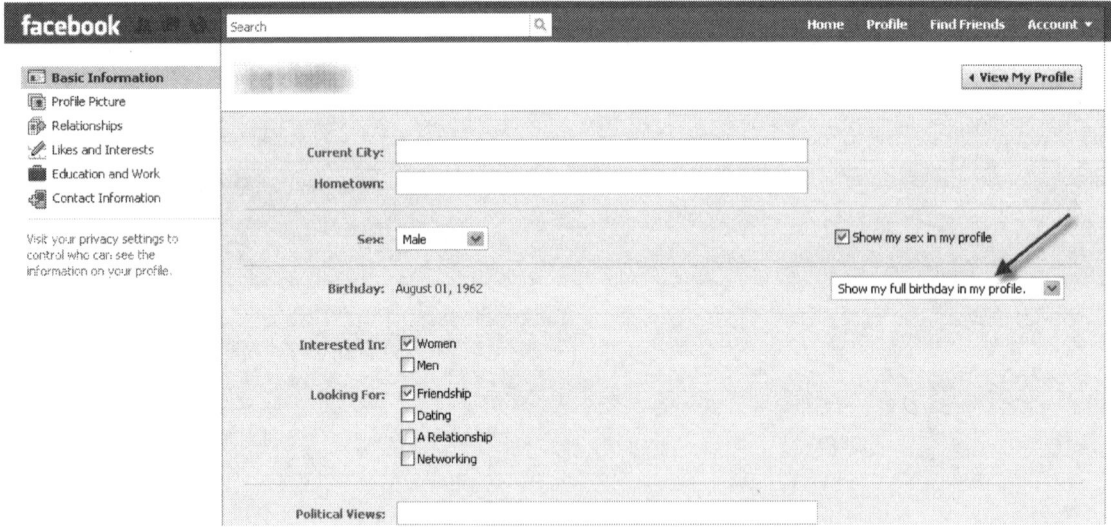

On this screen, you can enter information such as your hometown, birthday, political and religious views as well as your bio and favorite quotes. None of this information is required in order to have a profile, other than the date of birth; it is all up to you – enter whatever you feel comfortable with and want to share with others.

We do recommend that you NEVER show your full birthday in your profile. This is the kind of information that is perfect for identity thieves to have. Facebook's default setting is to "show my full birthday in my profile." To change this, click on the drop down arrow and change it to "show only month and day." If you don't want your birthday to show up at all, change it to "Don't show my birthday in my profile." This is an important piece of information you'll want to check on your children's profiles as well to make sure they don't share their birth year signaling to the entire world their exact age. Because Facebook is a "social" network, many people enjoy having their birth month and date visible to friends. It's a lot of fun to receive birthday greetings and wishes on your special day. Not only will you enjoy hearing from friends and relatives, but they enjoy being reminded that it's your birthday and given a

chance to wish you well. This is one of the many ways in which Facebook encourages social interaction.

```
Relationship Status:  Your relationship with ____ will be canceled upon saving.
                      [ Married ▼ ] to
                      [   ] [_____]

Family Member:        [   ] [_____]
                      [ Select Relation: ▼ ]
                                                    Remove

                      Add another family member

                      [ Save Changes ] [ Cancel ]
```

On the Relationships screen, you can enter information such as your relationship, add in your partner's name and link it to your partner's profile, add in your anniversary date and link to your children's and family members profiles. Again, none of this information is required; it is completely to your discretion. We do not recommend you add young family member's names to your profile especially those of younger children.

If you have been on Facebook previously, and have added "Likes and Interests" to your profile, the next screen to view and

Facebook® Guide for Parents 26

© SupremeSocialMedia.com

update is the Likes & Interests page.

Lisa McKenzie

Activities:	What do you like to do?
	I love eating corn flakes early in the m
	Spending Time With My Family
	I love eating corn flakes early in the morning while watching the sun rise from my condo in Boca
Interests:	What are your interests?
	Social media, Social change, Random Acts of Kindness
	Social media
Music:	What music do you like?
	Paula Cole, Lilith Fair, Susan Boyle, Andrew Brown, Sam Tsui, Mookie Morris, Sarah McLachlan, Mikey Wax Music, Jason Mraz, Alanis Morissette, John Mayer
	Paula Cole
Books:	What books do you like?
Movies:	What movies do you like?
	Walt Disney Studios Motion Pictures Cana, Save 2 Lives
	Walt Disney Studios Motion Pictures Canada

On this screen, you'll have the opportunity to share your likes, interests, favorite activities, etc. This is another way old friends will be able to find you and know that this is your profile. But, remember that all of this information will be available to your friends, friends of friends or whomever you decide to share your profile with based on your privacy settings. We will go through your privacy settings in detail further in this book.

© SupremeSocialMedia.com

The next screen to view and update is the Education & Work screen.

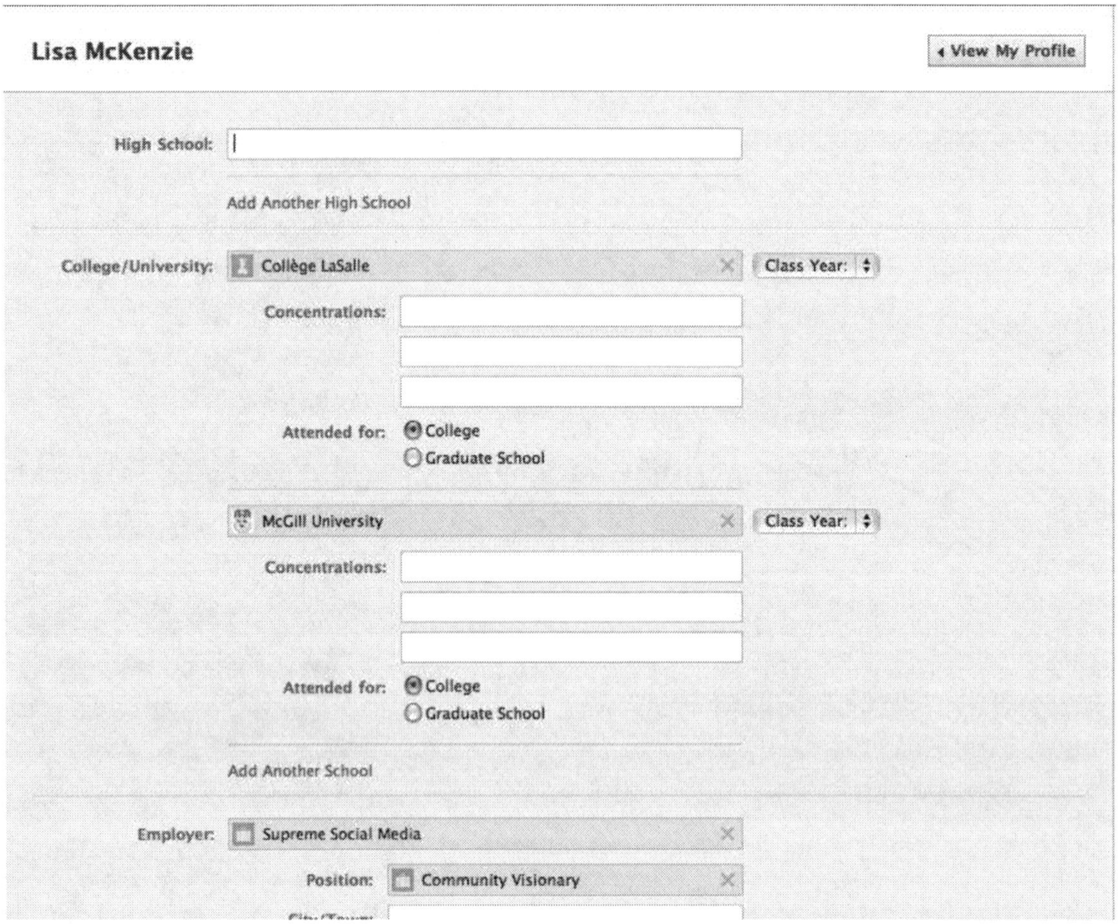

Lisa McKenzie ◂ View My Profile

High School: [ ]
Add Another High School

College/University: Collège LaSalle × | Class Year: ⇕
Concentrations: [ ]
[ ]
[ ]
Attended for: ● College
○ Graduate School

McGill University × | Class Year: ⇕
Concentrations: [ ]
[ ]
[ ]
Attended for: ● College
○ Graduate School

Add Another School

Employer: Supreme Social Media ×
Position: Community Visionary ×

Here's where you'll have the opportunity to add your High School, College and University details. Facebook also uses this information to suggest potential connections with other graduates from the same schools. If you feel comfortable sharing your work information, go ahead and enter it as well.

The next part of this section deals with your Contact Information:

```
Emails:
    Add / Remove Emails
IM Screen Name(s): [            ] Yahoo
    Add another screen name
Mobile Phone: [            ]
Land Phone:   [            ]
Address:      [            ]
City/Town:    [            ]
Neighborhood: [            ]
Zip:          [            ]
Website:      [            ]

[Save Changes] [Cancel]
```

We recommend that you do not enter all of your personal information. However, if you have a business website and you'd like to use Facebook to attract potential business clients, it can't hurt to post it here. But you may not want to include your full address and phone numbers for everyone to see.

There have been some high profile news stories about people posting their vacation plans on Facebook and then being robbed. While this is a rare concern, you wouldn't post your vacation plans on your front lawn. That's what it's like to include your full address, phone number AND tell the world through Facebook that you're away for a month and your guard dog is in the Heavenly Farms boarding house. It sounds absurd that people would be so willing to share such private details about their lives but we see it all the time and want to warn you about the risks. Sharing details about your life is what makes social networking social but at times children forget or dismiss the possible dangers and share too many intimate details. It's necessary to remind our children that some details about their and their family's lives are private and should not be shared on Facebook or any other social networking website.

We also want to draw your attention to the "email" area. Facebook defaults to showing your email address to "friends only." We recommend changing this setting to "Only Me" so that you do not open yourself up to receiving unwanted e-mail. We will cover that later under privacy settings. Again, this advice is for those of you using Facebook for personal pleasure. If you are considering using Facebook to attract business clients, you'll want to make it easy for those people to find you and listing your e-mail address will be a good idea. For personal use, friends can always send you a message using the message function within Facebook and do not need to have your e-mail address. Detailed instructions for setting your e-mail privacy choices are provided in Chapter 5.

We're now done with editing your profile, let's move on to Account Settings.

Chapter 3: Account Settings

In this chapter we'll review your Account Settings, which covers the overall configuration of your account, name, user Id etc, as well as some additional things such as notifications and language. You can access the Account settings from the drop down menu on the top blue navigation bar all the way to the right under "Account." We cover privacy in great detail in the next section.

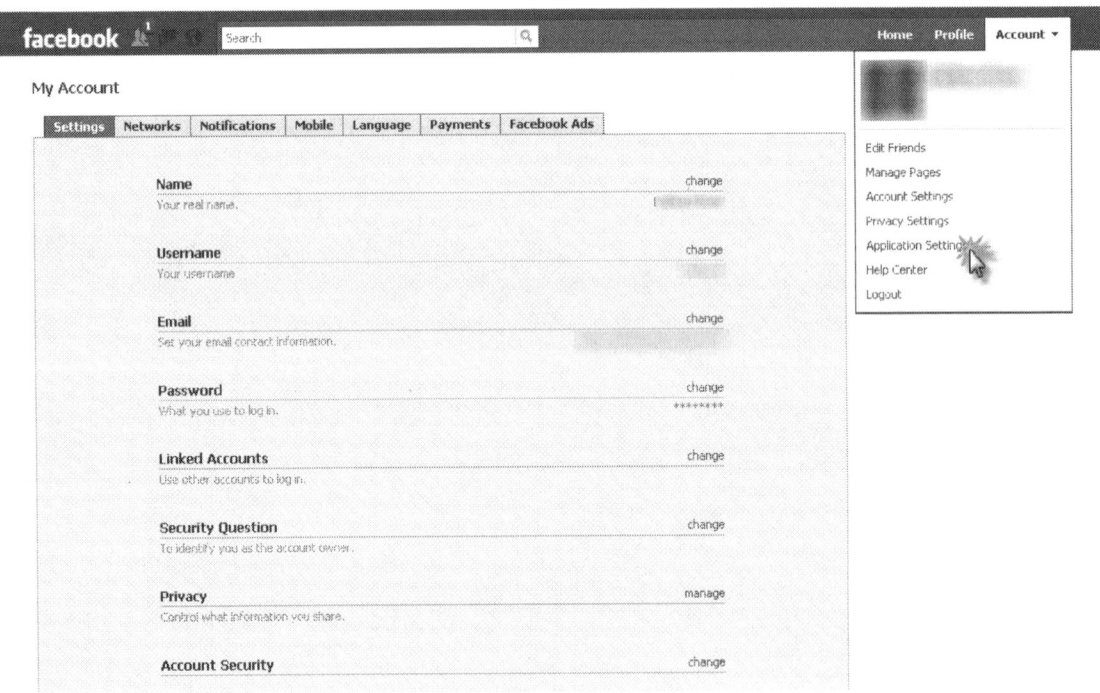

Once you are on your Home Page, which you'll access from the blue navigation bar, right hand side, top of the page, or your Profile, which you can find right next to "Home" on the blue bar, click "Account" on the blue navigation toolbar.

- In the dropdown menu select settings or "Account Settings".

- Click on "Settings" and make sure all of your information is correct.

- You can link your accounts under the Linked Accounts option but we suggest that you keep your Facebook account separate from other network to keep tighter security levels on your passwords.

- The other area we want to draw your attention to is the "Account Security" section:

Privacy	manage
Control what information you share.	
Account Security	change
Deactivate Account	deactivate

This was a great feature added by Facebook that allows you to be notified if someone tries to access your account from a computer or mobile device that you have not used before. That way if someone is trying to "hijack" or "hack" your account, you will be notified. It works best if you have a text-message-enabled phone so you are instantly notified.

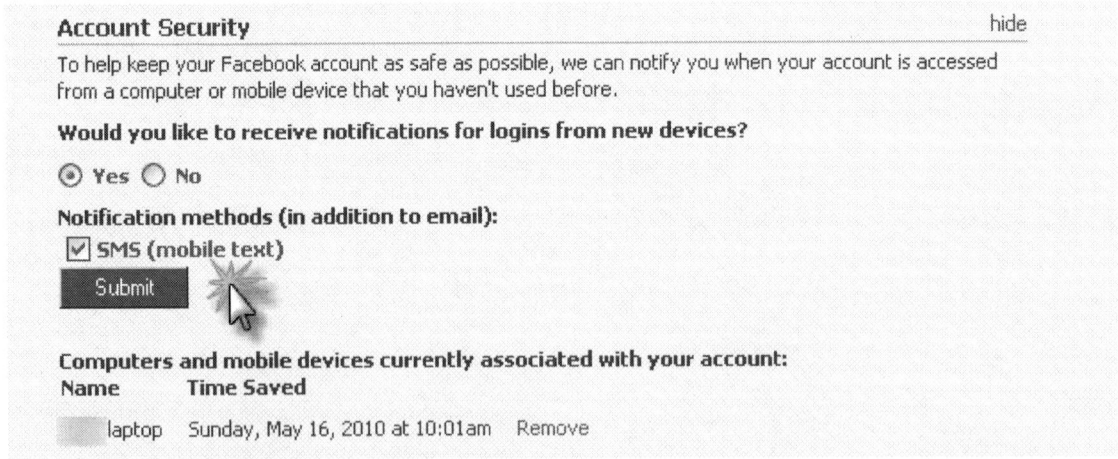

The Networks Tab:

The Networks tab will allow you to be added to a network of friends or classmates, if you would like. This will help friends, former classmates or business colleagues find you on Facebook.

We recommend you speak to younger children and teens about leaving this area blank. If strangers know the name of your child's school or the town you live in, it can become easier for someone to find your child off line.

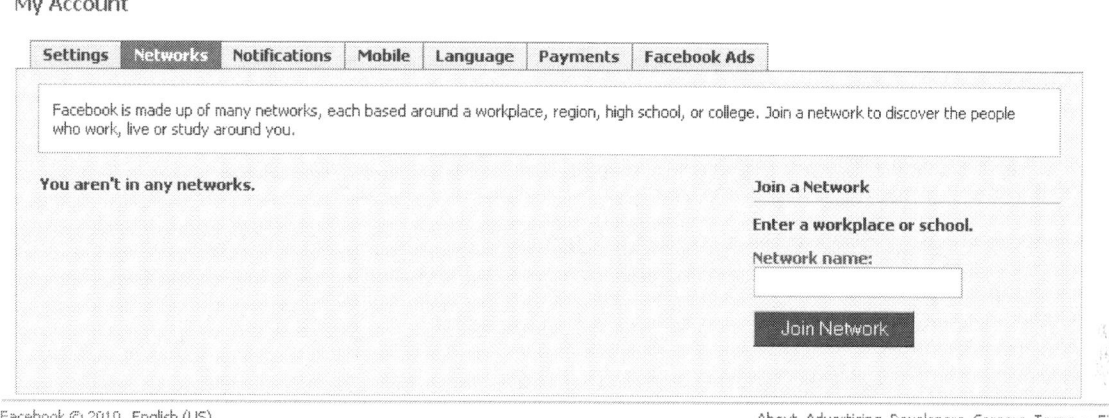

The Notifications Tab:

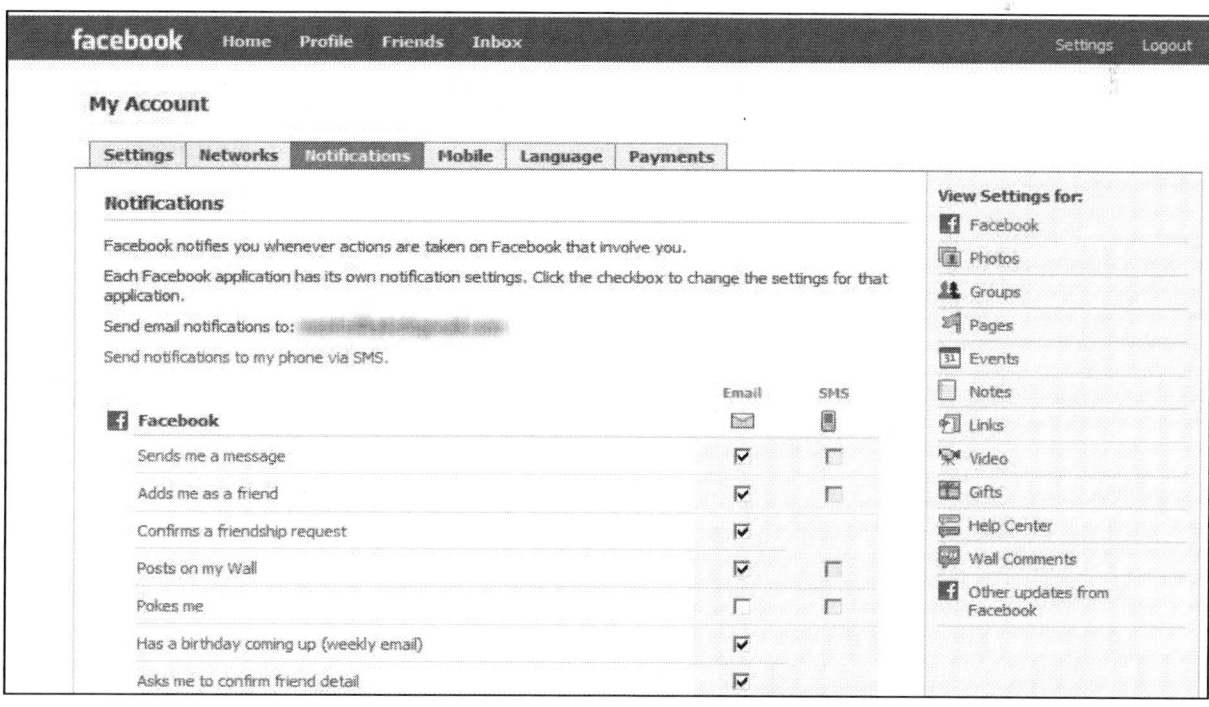

This is where you check off the access to your notifications of events, notices and the like. Checking the box allows, no check removes access.

We find it beneficial to receive immediate notifications of certain items while being notified of others can be annoying. This is just a basic screen shot but when you get to the screen, you can see how granular it can become. You can always come back to this screen and change these settings as you find out how many e-mail notifications you are receiving.

You can even go so far as having notifications sent to your cell phone via SMS or Text message. This is something you definitely want to discuss with your child. It could get expensive if you do not have a text message plan. You want to avoid excessive text messaging charges and Facebook messages can really build up fast. This is a nice option if you have unlimited text messages on your mobile plan but otherwise, as with all text messaging issues, beware. Kids text and chat a lot; not just on their mobiles but on Facebook as well.

Mobile Tab: This is where you can register for mobile texts. It also verifies your information. You can "subscribe" to a users

profile via SMS or text messages and be sent a text message every time your child posts an update to their wall.

This may be a feature you would like to use to check in on your child. Again, verify to make sure you have a text plan before enabling this or your mobile bills could increase.

Language Tab: Facebook is now available in more than 70 languages. If you would like to use your native language to view and interact on Facebook, you can set it here.

Payment Tab: You can make purchases via Facebook but mostly people use this for purchasing Facebook advertising. We recommend that you set this up only if you would like to purchase Facebook ads for business.

Facebook Ads Tab: This is where Facebook could use your personal information for Facebook social ads. Although Facebook says here they will not use your photos in ads, we recommend that you set this to "no one".

Also, Facebook lets your friends know when you've "liked" an ad, you may not want that to be shown so scroll down to the bottom and select "no one" as well.

Chapter 4: Privacy Settings Profile Information

The question we get the most when we are out speaking to organizations, schools and parents about Facebook is "what should I be aware of in order to protect my privacy and my child's privacy while using Facebook?"

Facebook offers a very detailed privacy platform and with the information outlined in these chapters, you can now go over both your settings and those of your children and set those controls to suit your comfort level.

As we mentioned, the "Privacy Settings" screen is accessible from both the "Account Settings" screen and the "Privacy Settings" areas.

To access the "Privacy Settings" screen go over to the upper right hand corner of your Facebook profile on the blue navigation bar and click on the "Account" tab and choose "Privacy Settings."

© SupremeSocialMedia.com

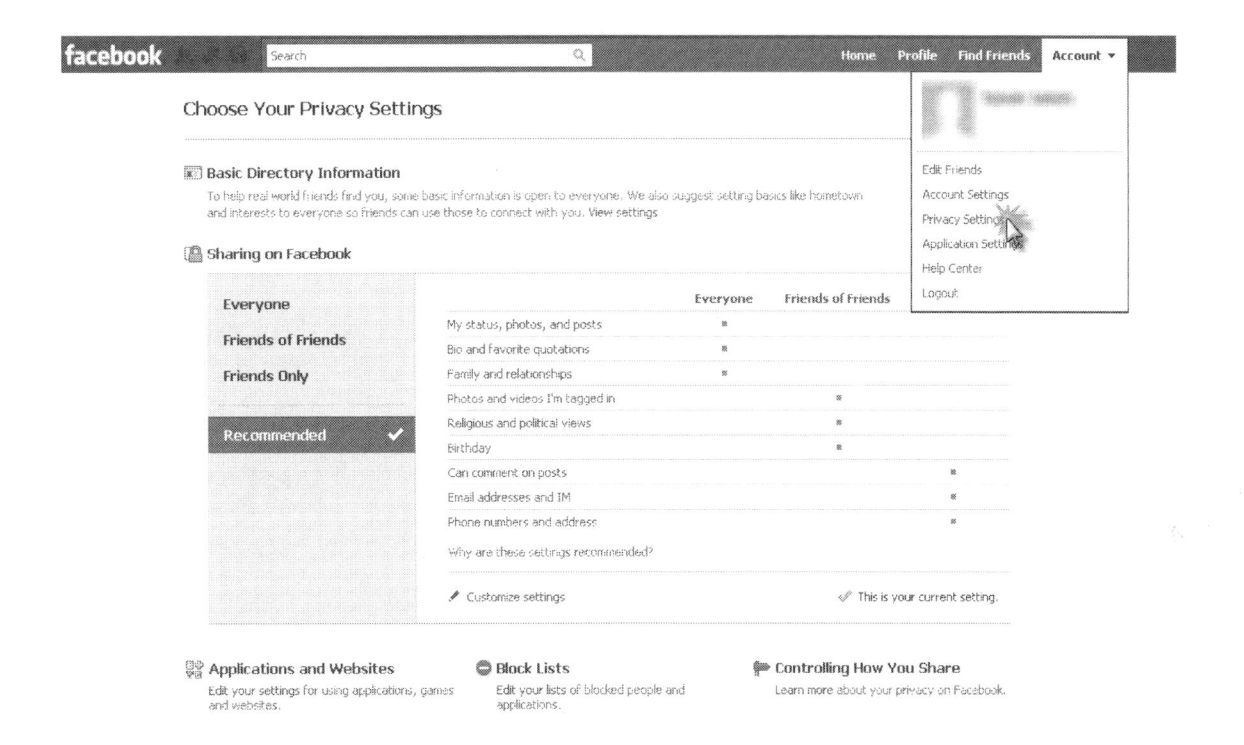

As you can see, Facebook defaults most of your settings to those that are the least private. Here is a detailed explanation of the main 3 privacy settings.

1. **Everyone – This is not just everyone on Facebook, this is everyone on the INTERNET. This information is indexed by Google's search engine as well other search engines. Facebook says,** "the "Everyone" setting works differently for minors (under 18) than it does for adults. When minors set information like photos or status updates to be visible to "Everyone," that information is actually only visible to

their friends, friends of their friends, and people in any school or work networks they have joined. That's still a lot of people to view their personal photos and updates. We highly recommend that you check these settings and make sure they are not set to "everyone" for your child's profile. Most likely Facebook's own blocking system is protecting your child but why take a risk. IF your child were to fake his or her birth date (and this happens more than we'd all like to think) on Facebook, all of these things would become visible to everyone.

2. **Friends of Friends – This means all of the people you "friended" AND <u>all</u> of <u>their</u> friends.** Many people do not understand what this means so we want to be clear. Let's say you have not "friended" your boss but you have "friended" a co-worker who HAS "friended" your boss. If you have your settings configured to 'friends of friends' your boss will be able to see that area of Facebook. If your "wall" settings are set to 'friends of friends' and you make a post about how much you hate your boss, he or she will be able to see it. Now might be a good time to remind you that what you post on Facebook should always be considered to be public, no matter what your

privacy settings are set to. Use common sense and don't post things you wouldn't want others to see.

3. Only Friends – The means that only people you "friend" can see your profile information.

You also have the option to "Customize Settings"

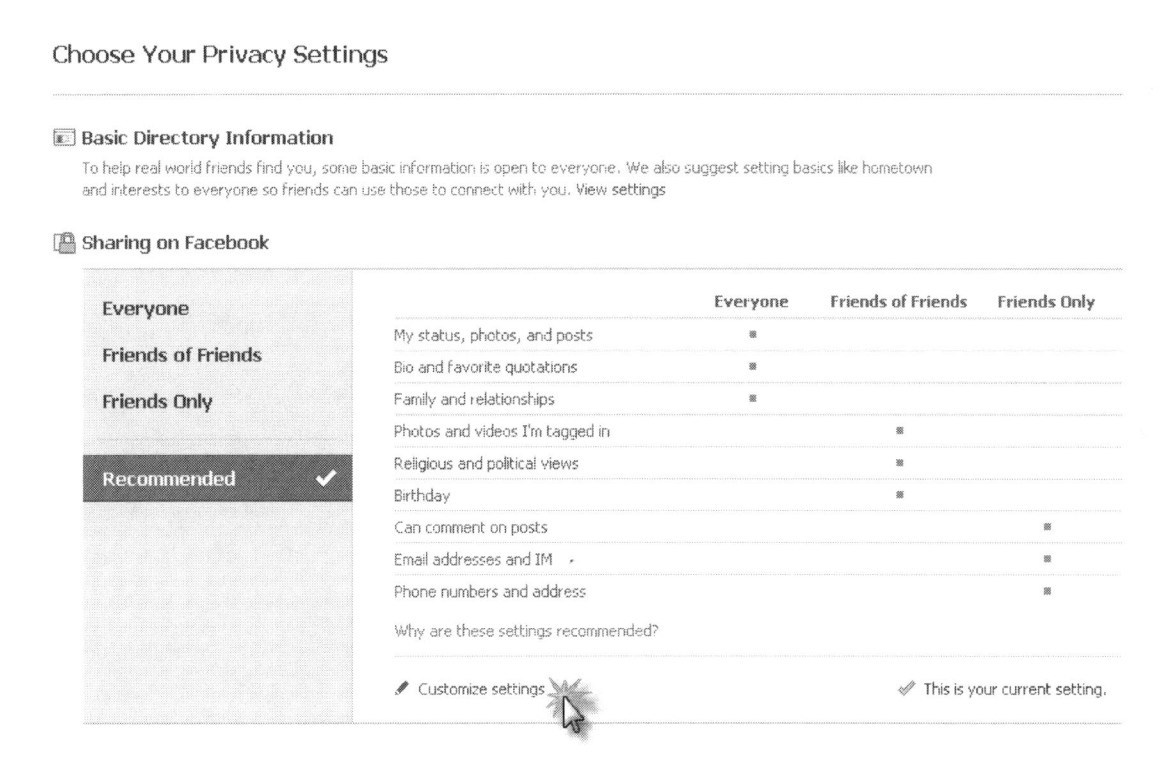

Choose Your Privacy Settings

Basic Directory Information
To help real world friends find you, some basic information is open to everyone. We also suggest setting basics like hometown and interests to everyone so friends can use those to connect with you. View settings

Sharing on Facebook

	Everyone	Friends of Friends	Friends Only
My status, photos, and posts	■		
Bio and favorite quotations	■		
Family and relationships	■		
Photos and videos I'm tagged in		■	
Religious and political views		■	
Birthday		■	
Can comment on posts			■
Email addresses and IM			■
Phone numbers and address			■

Sidebar options: Everyone / Friends of Friends / Friends Only / **Recommended** ✓

Why are these settings recommended?

✎ Customize settings   ✓ This is your current setting.

If you click customize, you will be taken to this screen that has these and other privacy choices:

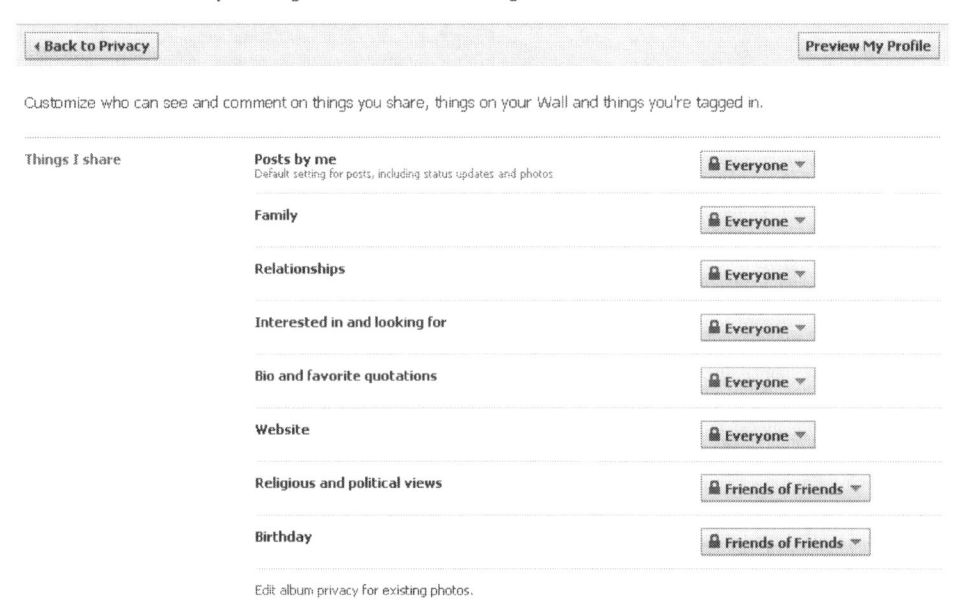

If you click on the drop down box next to each of the choices you can "customize" further your exposure:

Once you click on "customize" on this screen you will see that the phrase "Hide this from" is a choice. Here, you can manually select friends that you would like to exclude.

Facebook® Guide for Parents 42

© SupremeSocialMedia.com

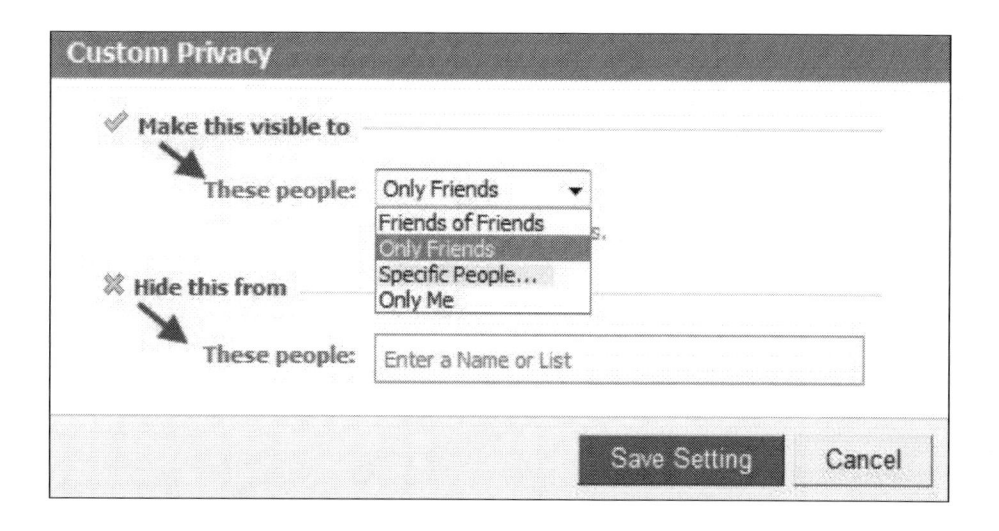

Using the "posts by me" setting as an example, customizing this setting might be useful if you post often about your child's soccer games and this information is not interesting to your co-workers. It might also be used to hide information about a surprise party from the guest of honor. But if you find you are regularly hiding posts from the same people because you don't want them to know what you are doing, then you might consider simply "unfriending" them. They won't be notified when you drop them from your friend list. The only way they can confirm that you have unfriended them is if they view your profile and the option to "Add as Friend" is available. In other words, if they can now friend you, they are no longer a friend.

Towards the bottom of this screen there is an option "Allow friends to post on my wall." Make sure that this is checked off to allow your friends to post on your wall and connect with you. If it's not checked they will not be able to leave you messages and your page will be a stagnant page with just your posts.

In addition, you can check how your Profile looks to other people—**and we highly recommend doing so**—by clicking on the Preview My Profile link in the upper right hand corner of the screen (see below).

Choose Your Privacy Settings ▸ Customize settings

◂ Back to Privacy		Preview My Profile
Customize who can see and comment on things you share, things on your Wall and things you're tagged in.		
Things I share	**Posts by me** Default setting for posts, including status updates and photos	🔒 Friends Only ▾
	Family	

This will show you how *most people* (in Facebook's words) will see your profile when they visit you. You'll be able to double check how you've set your profile and correct any oversights. One of our partners, a very experienced Facebook user, checked "preview my profile" and discovered that she'd left her home phone number visible to "everyone." Yikes.

Remember, you can always come back to this same spot, make changes and adjust.

It is especially important for you to do this with your child. Double check his or her profile using the "preview my profile" button and talk to them about what they share with the world.

In many cases we recommended that you don't even fill out any of this information, i.e. interested in and looking for, family, relationships etc. but especially your children do not. There is no reason they need to tell people their all of this information but if you did you may want to go in here and customize your settings.

A couple of areas we want to draw your attention to:

Bio or favorite quotation:

The section under your profile picture called "About Me" or "write something about yourself" on the profile page. We suggested you take a moment and fill out this area when you created your Facebook profile. This is where you can tell people about you, your business if you have one or your personal blog, and share your website information. This information can be updated or changed whenever you choose. Have fun with this area and feel free to share hobbies, interests, a quote that means something to you or a philosophy. Again, you can change this information as often as you like so have fun. You may want to leave this as "everyone" so people who search for your profile can find out more about you. Or if you have a business website and would like to help potential customers or client find out more about you and your business quickly, you can make your website URL "clickable" from this area. To make your website address clickable, format it this way: http://yourwebsite.com using the http:// and NOT just www.yourwebsite.com. This is a nice feature and encourages people to find out more about you and your business, charity or other interest you'd care to share.

Edit Photo Album Privacy:

Religious and political views	🔒 Friends Only ▼
Birthday	🔒 Friends Only ▼

Edit album privacy for existing photos.

You will also have the opportunity to set a different privacy level for your photos on Facebook. In fact, you can set a different privacy level on each one of your photo albums, individually, once you upload your photos and create photo albums. This is a great feature because you will be able to share your "family" albums with your family, friend albums with your Facebook friends, and keep personal albums private from the view of your business Facebook friends, if you wish.

Relationships:

Things I share		
	Posts by me Default setting for posts, including status updates and photos	🔒 Friends Only ▼
	Family	🔒 Friends Only ▼
	Relationships	🔒 Friends Only ▼
	Interested in and looking for	🔒 Friends Only ▼

The likelihood is that your child will experience the ups and downs of teen relationships. It is also highly likely that they will "friend" someone they don't know well or that they don't know at all. Sometimes we see an example of a person changing their relationship to single, that status change goes out into the live feed and can be seen by others. Then they get messages from friends and friends of friends, asking them for dates, etc.

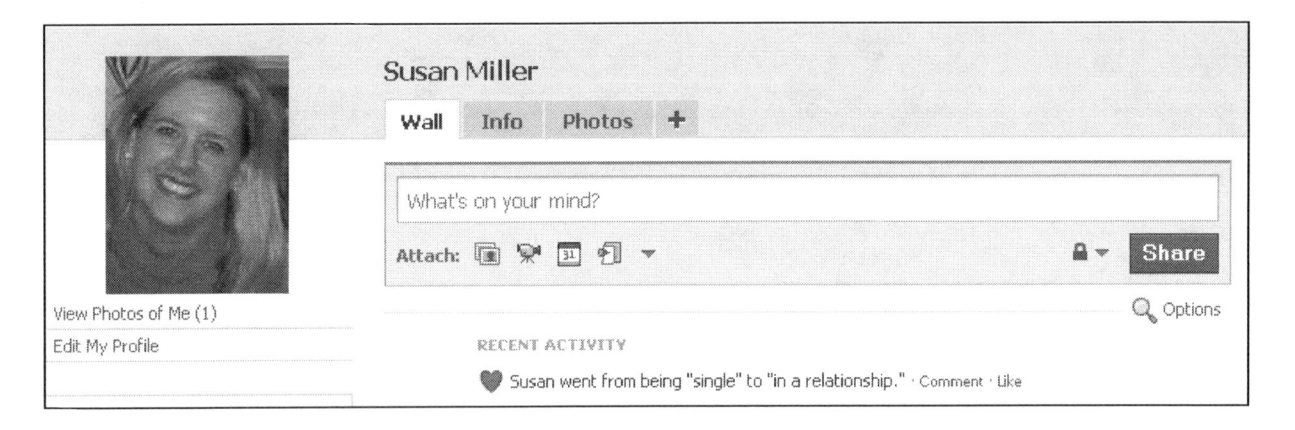

Also, this public breaking up can cause some anger in the person who is the one being left behind. This can be a very sore point with teenagers and can lead to cyber bullying, hurt feelings, jealousy and other stressful situations your child doesn't need. We feel it is wise to advise your child not to advertise his or her relationship status.

We recommend that your child doesn't even say that they are in a relationship in the first place, but if they do this can ensure that no one sees that it has changed.

To make these notifications private, scroll down and set the Relationship area to "only me" By clicking on Customize and selecting "only me" in a pop up window. This means that only your child will be able to see their relationship status update change.

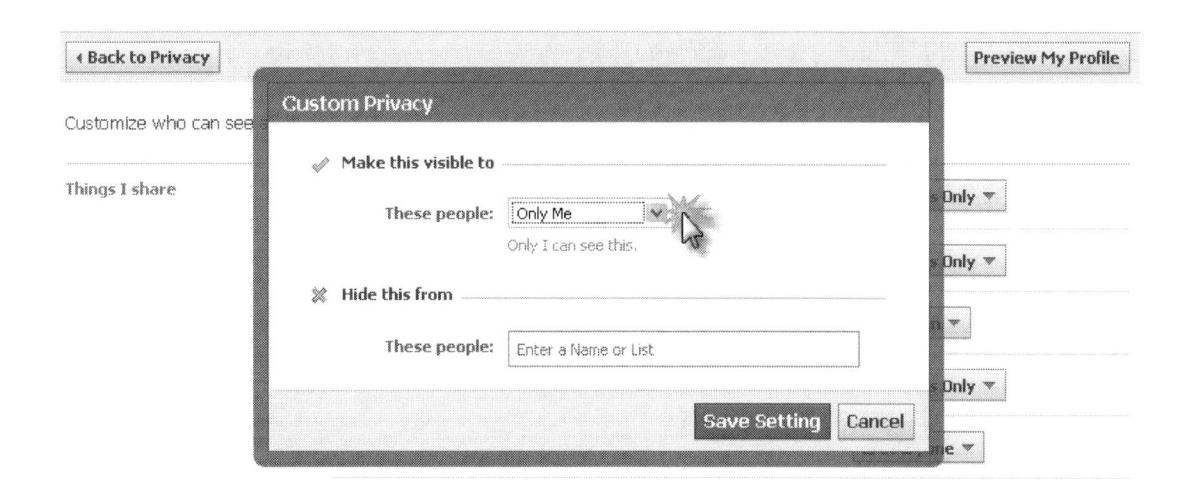

Photos and Videos I'm tagged in:

Think big hair and leg warmers...

Some of us use our personal Facebook profile for business and others have office friends that we've "friended" or parents of other children that we have "friended" and we really don't want to see our college spring break pictures online.

This privacy setting is very important. You can make sure if people post photos of you or your child and "tag" you or them in it, the photo does not get automatically posted into your news stream or profile. "Tagging" is a way for your friends to identify you in a post or photo AND to notify you that they've posted something that might be of interest to you or that includes you, such as pictures. When a photo is tagged, it appears in your news stream and profile for all of your friends to see unless you've set your privacy settings to avoid this.

Now you can't stop friends and relatives from posting unflattering, silly or embarrassing photos of you if they insist on doing so despite your protests, BUT IF the photo does get posted and you wish it didn't, you can certainly "untag" yourself so that at least the photo is not identified with your name and doesn't show up on your Facebook profile. To do this, find the picture you've been "tagged" in and beside your name, click on "remove tag" and this picture will no longer be linked to your profile on Facebook. Again, the photo will not be deleted from Facebook, only from your profile. We will cover tagging in a chapter later in this book and go into more detail.

As displayed in this screenshot, people can see your photos by either clicking View Photos of "friend's name" or clicking on the "Photos" tab on your wall.

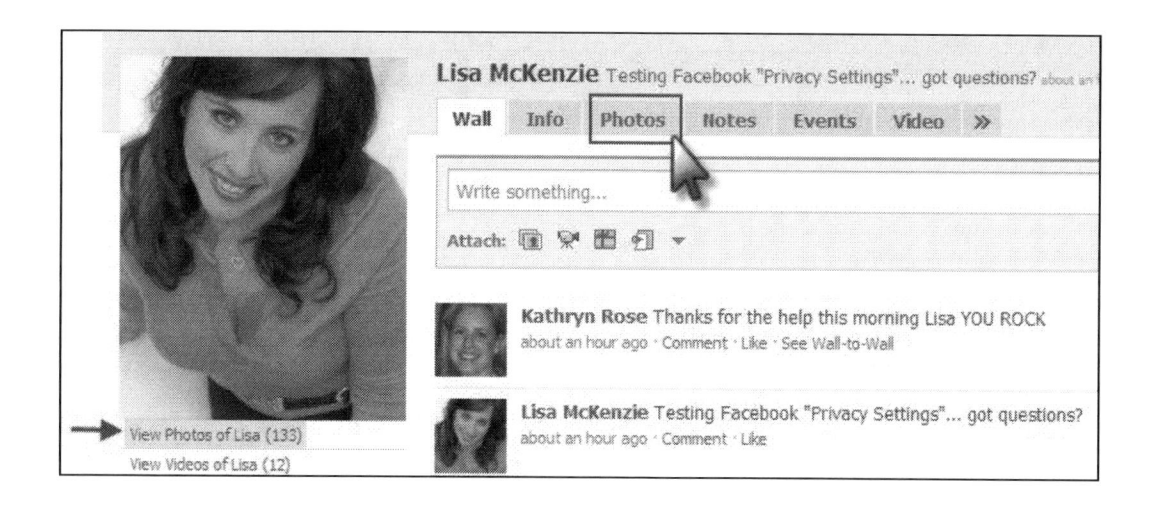

Here's an example of a photo tag gone wrong:

If you were Michael you might not want your current business colleagues or future college admissions officers to see this photo. (provided by the blog http://myparentsjoinedfacebook.com).

Get those photo privacy settings in place!

The rest of the choices are self-explanatory and we recommend you explore these on your own until you're comfortable.

Much like the "Relationship" area, go to the "Photos and videos I'm tagged in." Then click "Customize" and make sure it is set to "only me." This way if a photo is uploaded and tagged the only person who sees it is the profile owner, either you or your child.

Chapter 5: Privacy Settings - Contact Information

On the Facebook Customize privacy screen, if you scroll to the bottom, you will find the "Contact information area."

Contact information		
	Mobile phone	🔒 Friends Only ▼
	Other phone	🔒 Friends Only ▼
	Address	🔒 Friends Only ▼
	IM screen name	🔒 Friends Only ▼
	▓▓▓▓▓▓▓▓▓▓▓▓▓	🔒 Only Me ▼
	▓▓▓▓▓▓▓@earthlink.net	🔒 Only Me ▼

This area allows you to set the restrictions about who can who can see your contact information such as phone number, address, IM (Instant Message) Screen name (if applicable) and email address. Please remember our descriptions of what it means to share this information with "everyone," "friends of friends" or "only friends" and choose according to your comfort level. Again, you can change these at any time.

We do not recommend you make <u>any</u> personal information available for view to "Everyone." Also, our recommendation was, that unless you are using Facebook for business purposes, you don't even disclose this information in the first place.

One area we want to draw your attention to here is your email address. You may not mind if people you "friend" see your regular email address, but it might be a good idea for you to advise your children to set this to "only me" so that way if your child does friend someone they don't know, that person cannot reach out to your child through their primary email address.

To protect your e-mail privacy and your child's e-mail address, click on the drop down box, click "customize" then "only me."

However, if you have a business, it may be a good idea to list your business contact information and make that available to "everyone" along with your web address.

Chapter 6: Privacy Settings - Basic Directory Information

Choose Your Privacy Settings

Basic Directory Information
To help real world friends find you, some basic information is open to everyone. We also suggest setting basics like hometown and interests to everyone so friends can use those to connect with you. View settings

This area controls how you share some information. For instance, hometown, how people can find you on Facebook, and see what you "like" on and off Facebook.

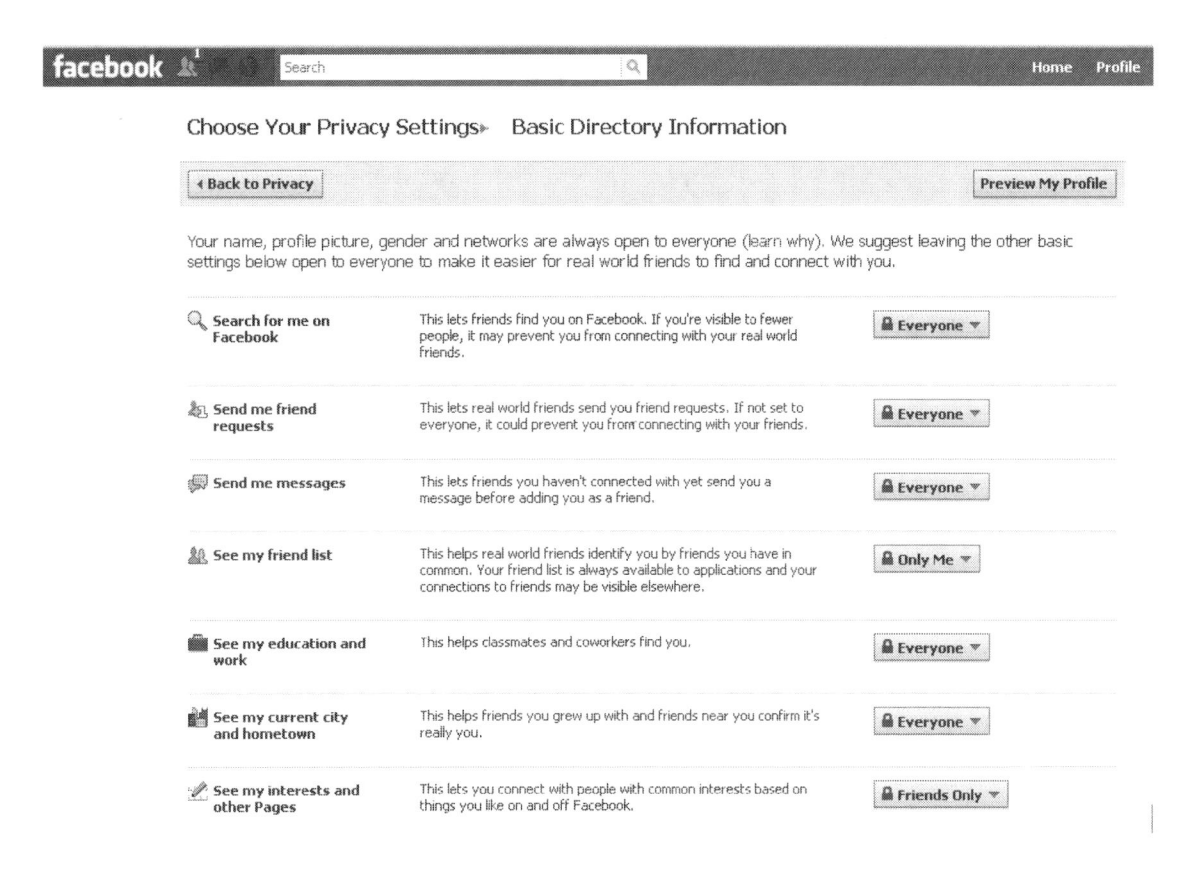

Choose Your Privacy Settings ▸ Basic Directory Information

◂ Back to Privacy   Preview My Profile

Your name, profile picture, gender and networks are always open to everyone (learn why). We suggest leaving the other basic settings below open to everyone to make it easier for real world friends to find and connect with you.

Search for me on Facebook	This lets friends find you on Facebook. If you're visible to fewer people, it may prevent you from connecting with your real world friends.	🔒 Everyone ▾
Send me friend requests	This lets real world friends send you friend requests. If not set to everyone, it could prevent you from connecting with your friends.	🔒 Everyone ▾
Send me messages	This lets friends you haven't connected with yet send you a message before adding you as a friend.	🔒 Everyone ▾
See my friend list	This helps real world friends identify you by friends you have in common. Your friend list is always available to applications and your connections to friends may be visible elsewhere.	🔒 Only Me ▾
See my education and work	This helps classmates and coworkers find you.	🔒 Everyone ▾
See my current city and hometown	This helps friends you grew up with and friends near you confirm it's really you.	🔒 Everyone ▾
See my interests and other Pages	This lets you connect with people with common interests based on things you like on and off Facebook.	🔒 Friends Only ▾

© SupremeSocialMedia.com

Facebook Internal Search

The first setting is "Search for me on Facebook". This automatically defaults to "Everyone" so you will have to go in here and decide by whom you would like to be found.

- ✓ Everyone
- ✓ Friends of Friends
- ✓ Only Friends

Search for me on Facebook	This lets friends find you on Facebook. If you're visible to fewer people, it may prevent you from connecting with your real world friends.	🔒 Everyone ▼ • Everyone Friends of Friends Friends Only
Send me friend	This lets real world friends send you friend requests. If not set to	

We recommend that you suggest to your child to set this to "Only Friends." This will completely remove them from the Facebook internal search engine so that the only people who can find them through search are those who ARE INVITED by them to be their friends. This means your child will have to invite people to be his or her friend on Facebook and not the other way around.

The reason for this is a simple one. It is easy for strangers to find young people on Facebook without even knowing them. For instance, if you type into the Facebook search bar a name like "Jane Smith," you will see a list of possible matches, with photos. If someone is interested in targeting young people, all they have to do is type in a name, look at the pictures and then send a "friend request" to your child. It's like looking through a yearbook in high school or a freshman face book in college (where do you think the name came from?).

Friend Requests and Private Messages

You may also wish to allow people to be able to "friend" you and send you a private message, however you may not want this option for your child, especially for younger teens.

| Send me friend requests | This lets real world friends send you friend requests. If not set to everyone, it could prevent you from connecting with your friends. | Everyone ▼ |
| Send me messages | This lets friends you haven't connected with yet send you a message before adding you as a friend. | Everyone ▼ |

If your child's profile is available for searches within Facebook once someone finds them, they can by default, either send them a friend request or send them a private message.

You may want to allow people to be able to "friend' your child but you may not want perfect strangers to be able to send them messages.

To turn off this ability for everyone to send your child a private message, find the area that says, "send me messages" and change it to "friends of friends" or better yet to "only friends."

Friends:

| See my friend list | This helps real world friends identify you by friends you have in common. Your friend list is always available to applications and your connections to friends may be visible elsewhere. | 🔒 Only Me ▼ |

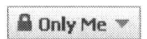

Facebook defaults to showing your friend list to "everyone." This may be something you want to consider limiting for your child. When the world can see all of your child's friends, then you have limited control over information about your child on the internet. If your child's privacy settings are set tightly but his friend "Bobby" shows information to "everyone" and posts about going to Lincoln Junior High School's basketball game every Friday night, strangers who are motivated can put bits of information together by using a string of posts and "see" where your child is located in the real world and what their habits are. We don't mean to be alarmist, but just realistic. Facebook is a very big playground. Help your children be safe.

To change who can view your friend list, click on the drop down menu to the right of "See My Friend List" and choose your own level of comfort, keeping in mind what it means to share with "everyone."

The other areas are pretty self explanatory but the last thing we want to draw your attention to is the "See my interests and other Pages".

This was added after Facebook gave the ability to add "like buttons" across the web. For instance, you could be on a news website and "like" an article. If you are logged in to your Facebook account, that information will be broadcast through your "newsfeed." This may or may not be something you want to restrict.

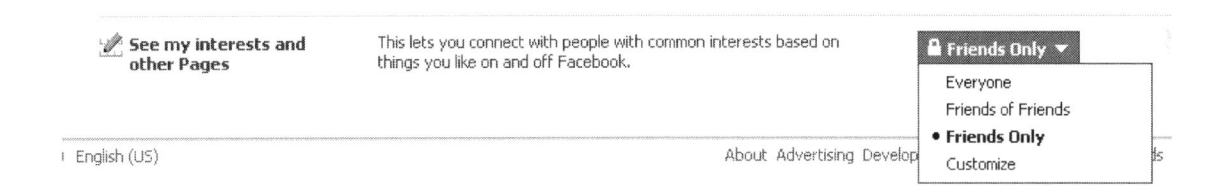

See my interests and other Pages	This lets you connect with people with common interests based on things you like on and off Facebook.	🔒 Friends Only ▼
		Everyone
		Friends of Friends
		• **Friends Only**
		Customize

English (US) About Advertising Develop

Chapter 7: Privacy Settings - Applications and Websites

In the Applications and Websites area under Privacy Settings, you can control what information is accessible to any applications you use, as they may publish stories in your Notifications and News Feed sections. As you make your profile settings more restrictive, less information is available to these applications.

This area also houses your "public search setting" that is how people can find your profile in a "Google" or other search engine search.

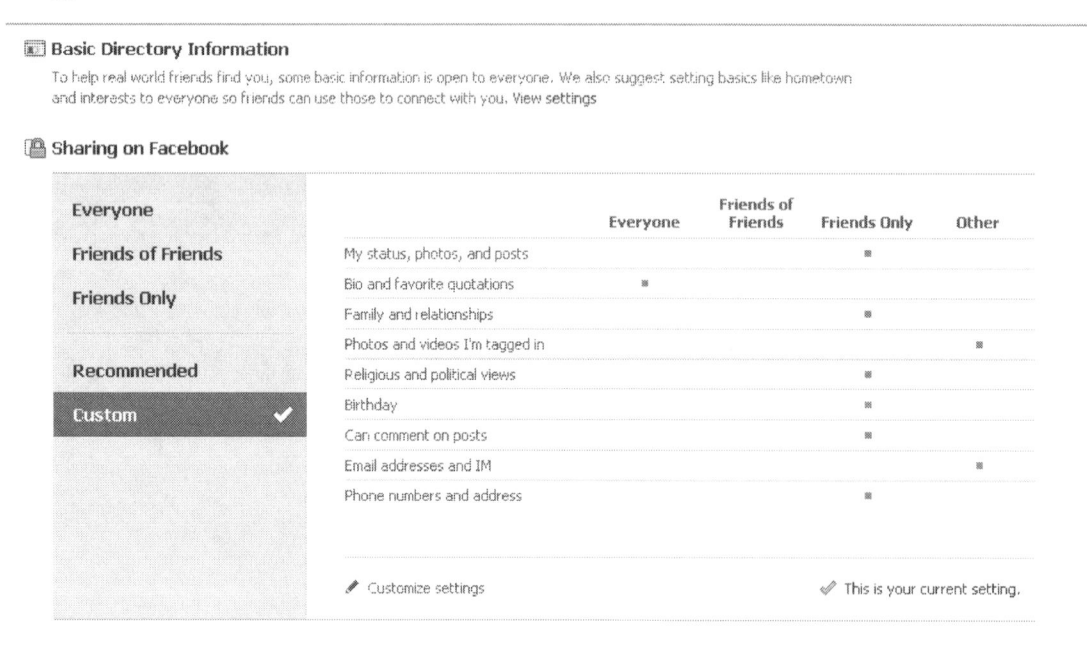

Once you click on "Applications and Websites, you will come to this screen:

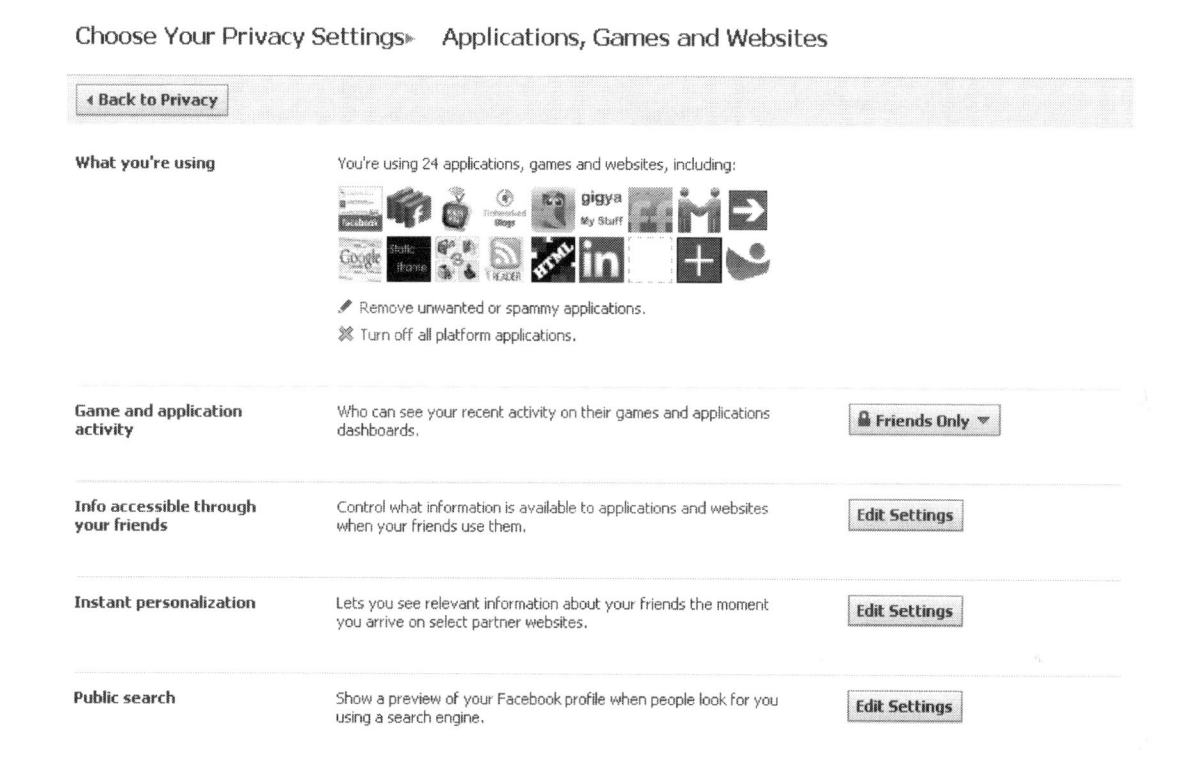

Choose Your Privacy Settings ▸ Applications, Games and Websites

◂ Back to Privacy

What you're using — You're using 24 applications, games and websites, including:

- Remove unwanted or spammy applications.
- Turn off all platform applications.

Game and application activity	Who can see your recent activity on their games and applications dashboards.	🔒 Friends Only ▾
Info accessible through your friends	Control what information is available to applications and websites when your friends use them.	Edit Settings
Instant personalization	Lets you see relevant information about your friends the moment you arrive on select partner websites.	Edit Settings
Public search	Show a preview of your Facebook profile when people look for you using a search engine.	Edit Settings

If you have been on Facebook previously, you may have a list of applications that you have used or have allowed access in the past. To remove them from your profile click "Remove unwanted or spammy applications." Or you can "turn off all platform applications. "

Facebook® Guide for Parents 61

© SupremeSocialMedia.com

To set restrictions on who can see your recent activity on games and applications, click on "Game and application activity." Here you can configure your settings as you like.

In the area that says "Info accessible through your friends," you will want to go through this and check the information that you want to allow your friends to share through the use of various applications on Facebook (like Birthday Calendar, or Greeting Card). Click on "edit settings" and you will come to a screen that allows you to control information that is shared.

Info accessible through your friends

Use the settings below to control which of your information is available to applications, games and websites when your friends use them. The more info you share, the more social the experience.

- [x] Bio
- [x] Birthday
- [ ] Family and relationships
- [ ] Interested in and looking for
- [ ] Religious and political views
- [x] My website
- [ ] If I'm online

- [ ] My status updates
- [ ] My photos
- [ ] My videos
- [ ] My links
- [ ] My notes
- [ ] Photos and videos I'm tagged in

Note: your name, profile picture, gender, networks and user ID (along with any other information you've set to everyone) is available to friends' applications unless you turn off platform applications and websites.

[Save Changes] [Cancel]

Facebook® Guide for Parents 62

© SupremeSocialMedia.com

The number of applications that are available can be overwhelming to say the least. Exercise caution every time you accept one. They often require permission from you to get all of your information as well as access to your friends information, and while you are having fun, the application is using that permission to track a variety of things about you and access your information!

These applications are free because using them gives them permission to gather information about you and your friends that make up offline profiles that are used as marketing data for the marketing arm of such companies. Un-clicking your personal information will still give your friends access to the application, the application will simply no longer have access to your information. In our opinion, the trade off of your friend playing a game should not be accessibility to your personal information.

We suggest you un-check all these items to keep your information yours. If you have any of your information set to "everyone" it will automatically be checked off on this screen.

Some applications are cool, like causes, others are fun like sending flowers and gifts, and others can be royal time wasters (for us things like mob wars, medieval knights, little green patches etc.). You'll decide through experience which ones you enjoy, and you can always delete any applications that you decide later you do not enjoy.

Some applications allow you to add information about yourself to your Wall and some will allow you to do special things. An application called Events will let you send an invitation to a specific activity to selected friends, and you might use this to set up a networking meeting or a party.

All of the games on Facebook are applications and if you find that you and your friends enjoy these, they are a nice way to interact with people. However, they can be annoying to others, so use at your own risk. If you find that you don't enjoy having people post news or requests for farm animals or Mafia connections on your page, you can block those applications so that friends can no longer send you requests to play those particular games. And you can remove any applications you've downloaded if you decide later not to use them.

A very popular Facebook application is the Birthday Calendar application. This alerts you when any of the people on your friend list has a birthday coming up. You can then go to their page and wish them happy birthday. The application will automatically ask you if you want to give a birthday gift, but you don't need to do that. Just click the "x" in the upper right hand corner of that box, get rid of the gifts option and write your happy birthday note in the space provided. This is a nice way to remember friends and colleagues on their special day and is one of the most used applications on Facebook.

The "Instant Personalization" setting

In April, 2010, Facebook introduced "Open Graph" application which they call "Instant Personalization." In our understanding, this is going to work much like amazon.com where once I log in to Amazon it shows me titles and products I may be interested in based upon past purchases. The idea is that users will want a personalized web experience so only content that matches their past likes will come up first.

What does this mean for you? Well, if you would like a more personalized experience than this will be great for you. The downside is this is an application and can collect personal information about you via the application or if your friends authorize the application it may collect information that way as well. For now, only 3 sites, Yelp.com, Pandora.com, and Docs.com have permission to do "instant personalization" in a beta test.

How do you turn off the personalization? You can go to the instant personalization setting and turn it off by unchecking the "allow" button. In our experience, this does not block the application from collecting information about you. You must go to the actual page and turn it off or say "no thanks". These three sites come up with a bar on the top saying "Hi Kathryn, Docs is using Facebook to personalize your experience. Learn More – No Thanks"

You can, however, decide what applications share about your personal information as we mentioned earlier by going to the "Info accessible through your friends" area and unchecking any information you do not want shared.

You can also prevent information from being shared by going back to all of the privacy settings and make sure that none of your settings are set to "everyone." Facebook says:

What you share when visiting applications and websites

Applications you use will access your Facebook information in order for them to work. For example, a review application uses your location in order to surface restaurant recommendations.

When you visit a Facebook-enhanced application or website, **it may access any information you have made visible to Everyone** *as well as your publicly available information. This includes your Name, Profile Picture, Gender, Current City, Networks, Friend List, and Pages. The application will request your permission to access any additional information it needs.*

What is the bottom line? Make sure your privacy settings are configured properly and do not share any information that you may not want accessed by applications. It is not necessary to divulge all of your personal information on Facebook.

Public Search Listing:

The last area we will focus on here is the "Public search" area.

| Public search | Show a preview of your Facebook profile when people look for you using a search engine. | Edit Settings |

This setting controls whether your Facebook profile comes up in a search engine listing like Google. In order to REMOVE yourself completely from Public Search Results (Google Indexing), simply click on the "edit settings" to the right of the "public search" area

Choose Your Privacy Settings ▸ Public Search

◂ Back to Applications

Public search — Public search controls whether things you've specifically chosen to share with everyone show up in searches on and off Facebook. It also controls whether people who enter your name in a search engine will see a preview of your Facebook profile. See preview

☑ Enable public search

and un-check "Allow" under the phrase "Public Search Results".

For children, Facebook states: "minors do not have public search listings created for them, so they do not appear in outside search engines until they have turned 18."

BUT we still recommend you check it for your child. Many children fudge their age on Facebook to appear older or to access things available only to adult users. While you may be vigilant about checking your child's profile, why take a risk.

You can see what your profile looks like in an internet search by clicking the "see preview" button, and again, we highly recommend checking out how your profile and your child's profile appear to the entire user base of the world wide web.

Facebook gets a huge amount of traffic from Google and the other search engines. Not all of your profile is displayed; only the information you allowed to be publicly shared when you set your privacy settings to "Everyone."

As you can imagine, this is an important feature to consider on your child's profile so that your child is not unintentionally showing all of his or her friends photos to everyone on the internet.

**Note: Potential employers or college admissions counselors have been known to do a "Google" search on prospective students or employees. Things posted on the internet live forever. In light of this, these settings are extremely important.

Privacy settings and joining groups or fan or community pages:

Joining groups, community pages and "liking" business fan pages are great ways to interact on Facebook. However, there are also privacy concerns here we want you to consider.

Even if your child's profile is private from people searching for them on Facebook, most groups and all fan pages are public.

If your child joins a group or "likes" a fan page that is public, they potentially open themselves up to being contacted by strangers.

Here is a real life example from one of the Supremes. "My niece told me about a person attempting to friend her by saying that they both play a popular game on Facebook. Since you only see your own Facebook friends while playing games, I went to investigate. It turns out she had joined a public group, and all a stranger in that group had to do was click on her picture to be able to send her a friend request. This is important for parents, and their children, to know." It bears repeating. Most groups, fan pages and community pages are public.

Chapter 8: Privacy Settings – Block List and Bullying

Unfortunately, our children, much like we were, are subject to the old saying, "kids can be so cruel." But online, the cruelest comments, videos and photos posted about them can haunt them forever. The impersonal quality of not being in the same room with each other can allow children to say and do things they might not say or do in person. They perceive an anonymity that does not exist and parental guidance in this area is a computer age challenge we need to address.

The first thing we recommend, of course, is that you really talk to your kids about the consequences of putting things online that are negative, downright mean or that don't present them in the best light. You want to be clear that you will not accept any behavior from your child that would be emotionally harmful to another child. In other words, you want to protect them from being bullied AND from becoming a bully. Both can be equally devastating to young lives.

If your child is being harassed, there are a couple of different things you can do, one is blocking users. Facebook gives you the option to actually block individual people from interacting with you. Of course, instead of "blocking" people, you can also always "unfriend" them. When you "unfriend" someone they do NOT get a notification about it. Only you will know that you "unfriended" them until they try to view your page. At that point they will realize they are no longer on your friend list. You can go to the privacy settings and click "block list." Add the person's name and they will be blocked--which ultimately means that your profile will no longer be visible to them when searching for you. Many people use this for ex-spouses and others they do not want to find them online.

You can also report a person who is bullying or harassing you or your child by clicking on "report this person" on their profile page.

The next thing we recommend is searching Facebook to look for potential Group or Page directed at your child. Some kids are setting up groups and pages with titles such as "I Hate Jane Smith." These are hateful ways to hurt others and your child might be so upset they don't tell you about them. Additionally you'll want to make sure that your child does not participate in any of these "hate" pages about other children. Take a look at your child's INFO tab on their profile to verify that the Groups and Pages they participate in are appropriate.

Go to the search bar and type in your child's name. Click on the magnifying glass to bring up all results. Then make sure to highlight "pages" or "groups." This will bring up the list of pages or groups that could have your child's name in the title. **<u>These pages and groups are against Facebook's terms of use and can be taken down so be sure to report them.</u>**

Here's how to report a page. Go to the offensive page and scroll to the bottom, then click report page Facebook will give you some choices about why you are reporting the page. Click the appropriate choice and then click "submit".

This is completely anonymous and your child doesn't even have to know you did it if you don't want them to.

Facebook also has some resources on the site to help you regarding child safety: Go to Account, then click on Safety and go to Help Center and follow instructions from there.

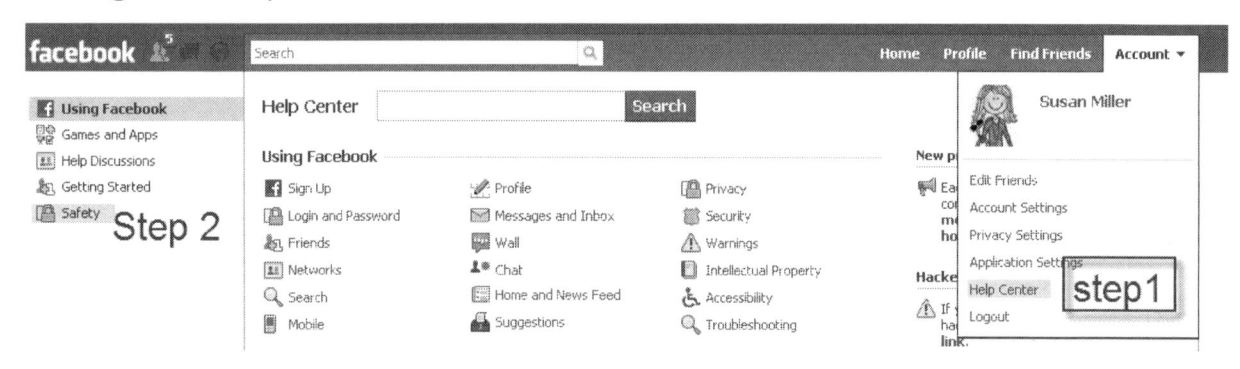

There are also, some great resources available on the internet that specifically focus on cyber bullying and we recommend you take a look at these sites. http://cyberbullying.us http://bullypolice.org. Facebook is a founding member of the StopCyberbullying Coalition http://stopcyberbullying.org

Every once in a while we search for pages we think are cruel and report them. We just think that Facebook should be fun for everyone and not a pulpit for spreading hate messages.

You also need to speak to your child about not bullying OTHERS; children, teachers or anyone else. In one of our searches for offensive content while writing this book, we found a page that said "I Hate Mrs. 'Jones.'" Of course this is just as hurtful to an adult as it is to children. Many states are putting laws on the books to punish cyber bullies. There is a case in Massachusetts where two teens are being prosecuted for "identity theft" for cyber bullying because they don't have a statute on the books that clearly speaks to online content. There have been some extremely high profile cases recently of children using social media sites to harass one another with fatal consequences. Children can be arrested and tried as adults in the most egregious cases. State and national laws are catching up to cyber crimes. You don't want your child to break the law or harm another human being. Children don't always understand the long-term consequences of their actions and need our help in this area.

We have more information on how to keep tabs on your child's online activities in the "reputation monitoring" section of this book.

Chapter 9: The Wall and News Feed

What is **The Wall**?

The Wall is the space on your Profile page you to use the publisher box to write "What's on your mind?" otherwise known as a "status update."

The wall also allows your friends to post messages and write notes to you.

What is the **News Feed**?

The News Feed is a flow of messages posted by your friends as well as yourself. Messages originate from people's profile Walls. Each message is stamped with the time and date the message was written and flows into the News Feed in its appropriate chronological order. Different users wall posts show up in the user's News Feed depending on their privacy settings.

Here is an example of what a News Feed looks like:

Your News Feed (visible if you click on the "Home" link on the upper right hand side of the blue navigation bar) is a collection of your friend's posts. The News Feed is Facebook's listing of posts by your friends.

There are two options as to which posts you view in your News Feed:

1. **"Top News"** is a selection of updates from your friends aggregated by Facebook using their own metric. It shows the posts from your friends that Facebook thinks are most

interesting to you based on your recent activity and the interactions you've had with your Friends, or Pages.

2. "**Most Recent**" is an actual real time chronological listing of all of your friends latest posts presented in the "live" stream of updates.

You can toggle back and forth to show the Top News or Most Recent.

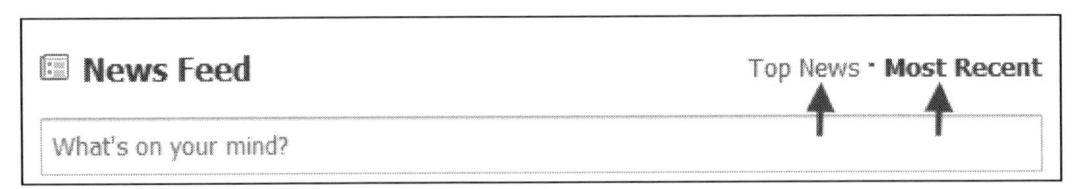

```
News Feed                           Top News · Most Recent
What's on your mind?
```

This is how you can keep in touch with your friends and find out what they're up to. You can post messages in response to their status updates to engage in conversation. Again, don't post anything that you want to be private.

Who's that writing on my WALL?

The Wall is the place where people can write notes to you. As stated above, you can also write on your own wall by simply creating a "status update" by writing something in the "What's on your mind?" publisher box.

Things written on your wall by you or others are PUBLIC, unless of course you change the privacy settings so beware.

Here are some embarrassing examples of Facebook posts gone wild (provided by the blog http://myparentsjoinedfacebook.com):

> Michelle ▶ Chris : LISTEN TO ME...PULL UP YOUR BOOT STRAPS AND STOP LETTING ONE CLASS GET YOU SO STRESSED AND INSANE ABOUT IT...THIS IS LIFE ,SOME THINGS COME EASY AND SOME YOU HAVE TO WORK AT...THIS IS ONE OF THEM THINGS . YOU WILL NOT GIVE UP ! YOU WILL DO IT AND GET IT OVER WITH! IM HERE TO HELP YOU..NOW DONT LET ME SEE ANOTHER THING ABOUT SCHOOL SUCKING!
> 5 minutes ago

> OMG I HATE MY JOB!! My boss is a total pervvy wanker always making me do ### stuff just to piss me off!! WANKER!
> Yesterday at 18:03 · Comment · Like

> Hi ###, i guess you forgot about adding me on here?
> Firstly, don't flatter yourself. Secondly, you've worked here 5 months and didn't work out that i'm gay? I know i don't prance around the office like a queen, but it's not exactly a secret. Thirdly, that ### stuff is called your 'job', you know, what i pay you to do. But the fact that you seem able to f###-up the simplest of tasks might contribute to how you feel about it. And lastly, you also seem to have forgotten that you have 2 weeks left on your 6 month trial period. Don't bother coming in tomorrow. I'll pop your P45 in the post, and you can come in whenever you like to pick up any stuff you've left here. And yes, i'm serious.
> Yesterday at 22:53

Below is an illustration by one of our Supreme Social Media partners of how "viral" a wall post can be:

"I write on Lisa's Wall – it shows up in her "news feed" as well as mine. Even if my privacy settings are set to allow only MY friends to see my wall, Lisa's may be set so that her friends, friends of friends AND their networks can see HER wall. Now my post is not private. It may be private for me, but not for Lisa."

Bottom line: if you're not sure who is going to see a post on your wall, don't post anything private. The ONLY way to ensure someone is getting a private message is to click on "Send Lisa a Message" under your friend's profile photo (see arrow).

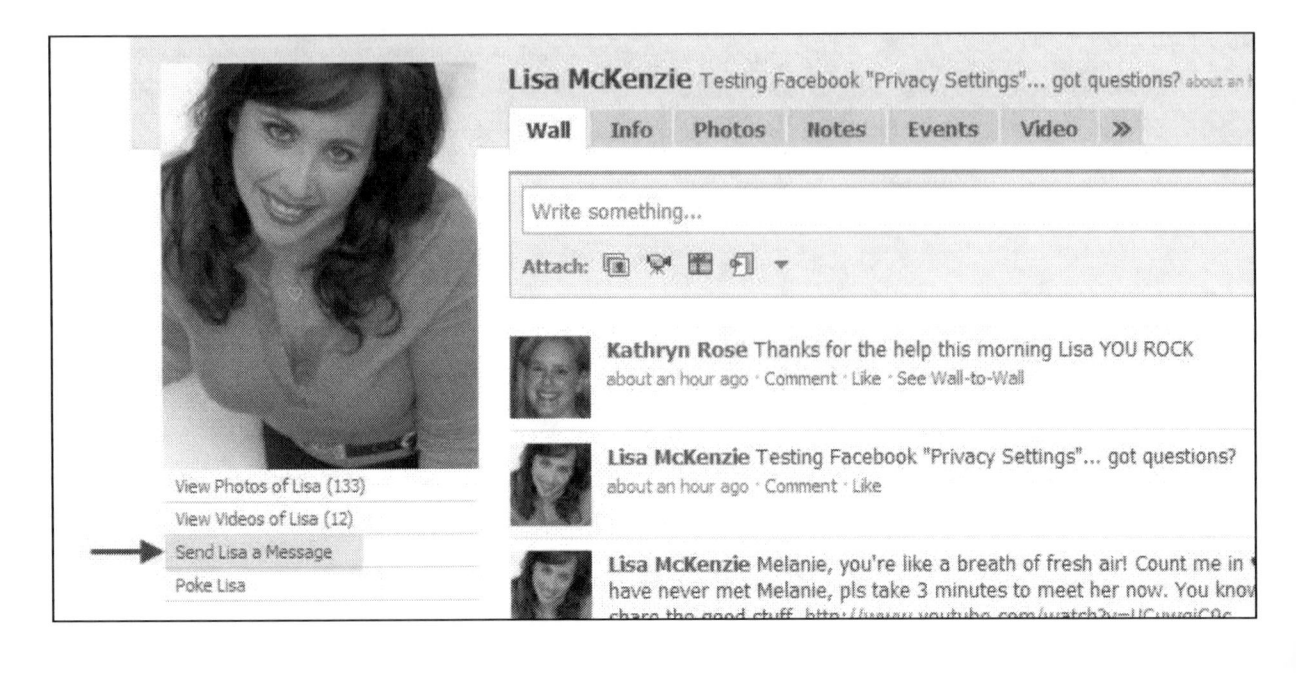

Facebook® Guide for Parents 80

© SupremeSocialMedia.com

You can control who can post to your Wall and who will be able to see those posts. Facebook has created couple of action steps for you to take.

Wall and News Feed: Privacy Setting

1. Right under your "status update field" is the "Options" button that controls which post will be displayed as default posts on your wall.

2. We recommend that you set this to "You + Friends" in order to create a storytelling atmosphere on your wall. If

you do not wish your Friends to see the posts made by other Friends, chose "Just You".

3. By customizing WHO can see the posts on your wall made by your friends, there is no need to block all users from writing on your wall. We recommend you check the option "Friends may post to my Wall," and under the option where you see "Only Friends," click on the pull down menu arrow until you see "Custom Privacy" option where you can use to make tighter selections.

Chapter 10: Finding People on Facebook

Whew, we are through with the privacy and profile settings. Fun, wasn't it? Not really we know, but necessary as you have no doubt discovered yourself.

Now the fun can begin. While being a little scary for newcomers, Facebook is a great resource to reconnect with old friends, reach out to new ones and start connecting with people. In our daily lives many of us wish we could be more connected. But with work, kids, pets, laundry, etc., it gets hard. Facebook provides us with a way to keep connected but only as much as we would like.

How do I find people? Start by finding people you know. Look up a long lost friend.

Simply type their name into the search bar and click the looking magnifying glass symbol on the right.

Once you have done this you will see some results :

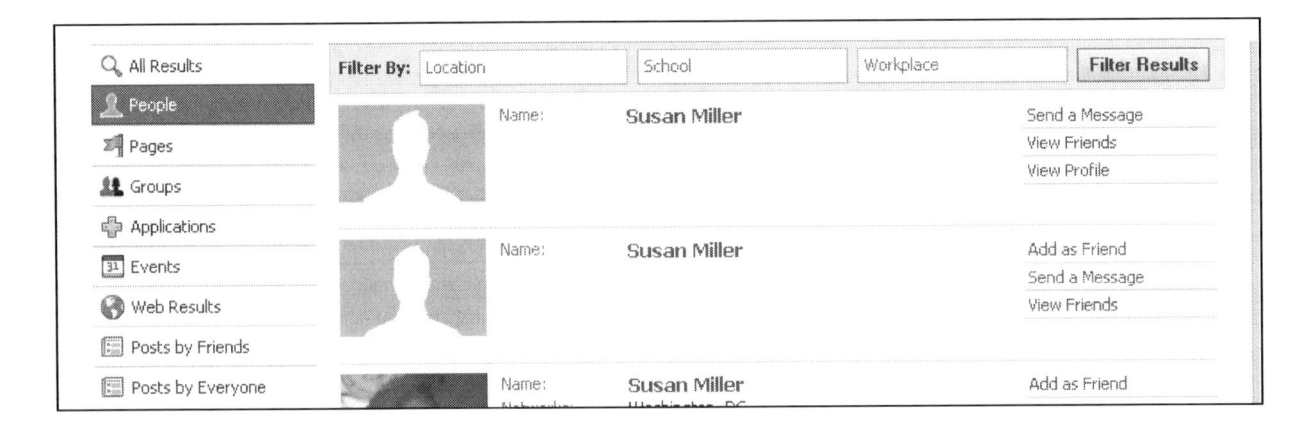

If the person has a common name like "Susan Miller," there can be a large number of results. So you'll want to filter by location, school or workplace and click "filter results."

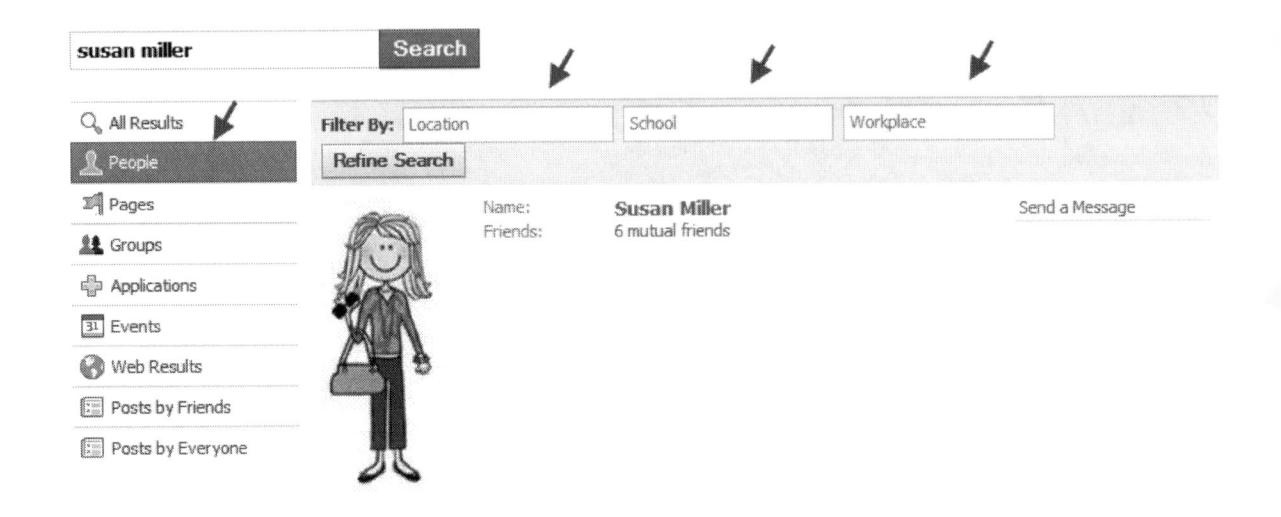

Once you start "friending" people, Facebook will start to recommend friends for you, based on your networks or friends you may have in common with other friends.

Another way to find friends is to go to the top of the navigation bar and click on "Friends Requests" icon:

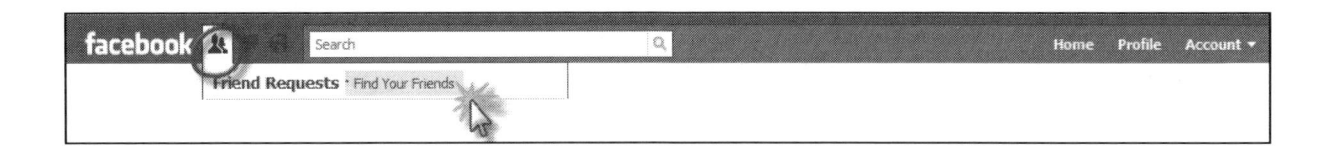

Click on "Find Your Friends" and you will come to a screen that allows you to upload your email contact list (not recommended if you have a mixture of personal and business contacts in your e-mail contact list), and Facebook suggests friends for you and allows you to search for people (see the image on the next page):

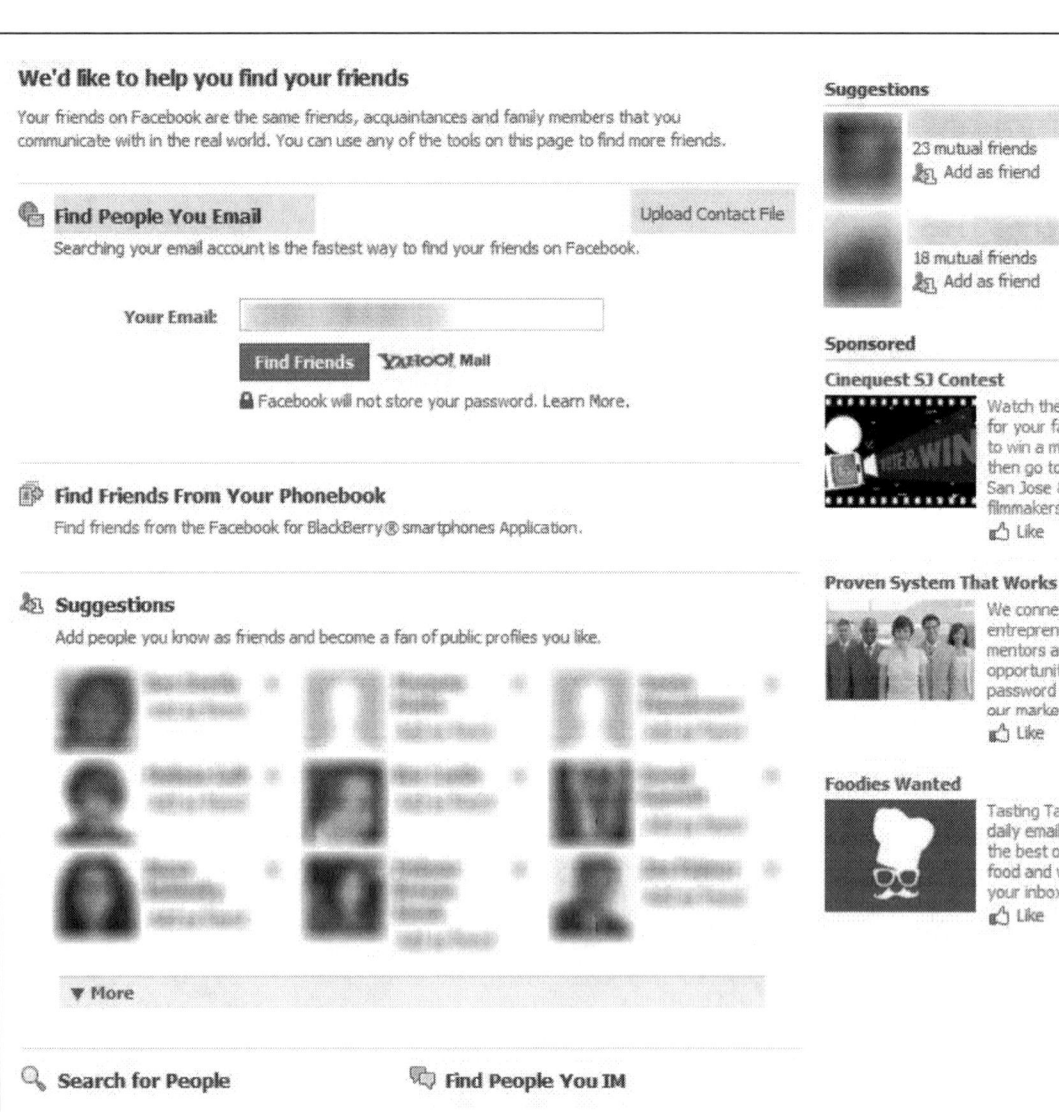

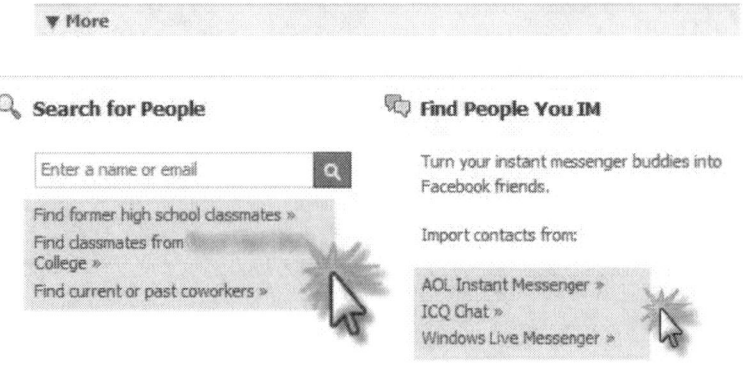

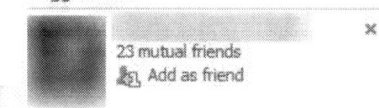

We'd like to help you find your friends

Your friends on Facebook are the same friends, acquaintances and family members that you communicate with in the real world. You can use any of the tools on this page to find more friends.

Find People You Email   Upload Contact File

Searching your email account is the fastest way to find your friends on Facebook.

Your Email: [   ]

[Find Friends] YAHOO! Mail

🔒 Facebook will not store your password. Learn More.

Find Friends From Your Phonebook

Find friends from the Facebook for BlackBerry® smartphones Application.

Suggestions

Add people you know as friends and become a fan of public profiles you like.

▼ More

Search for People

[Enter a name or email   🔍]

Find former high school classmates »
Find classmates from College »
Find current or past coworkers »

Find People You IM

Turn your instant messenger buddies into Facebook friends.

Import contacts from:

AOL Instant Messenger »
ICQ Chat »
Windows Live Messenger »

Suggestions

23 mutual friends
Add as friend

18 mutual friends
Add as friend

Sponsored   Create Ad

Cinequest SJ Contest
Watch the shorts, vote for your favorites & enter to win a microSDHC card, then go to Cinequest in San Jose & support indie filmmakers.
👍 Like

Proven System That Works
We connect entrepreneurs with mentors and opportunities. Use the password "guest" to view our marketing video.
👍 Like

Foodies Wanted
Tasting Table is the free daily email that delivers the best of the Bay Area's food and wine culture to your inbox. Sign up free.
👍 Like

Facebook® Guide for Parents 86

© SupremeSocialMedia.com

If you click on "Find former high school classmates" you come to this screen:

```
Classmate Search

    School Name:  [            ]        Class Year: [ ▼ ]
   Person's Name: [            ]
     (optional)

              [ Search for Classmates ]

Search by Company

        Company:  [            ]
   Person's Name: [            ]
     (optional)

              [ Search for Coworkers ]
```

Here, you can search by your school name and class year and also find people you work with or used to work with. It's a great tool for reconnecting with people!

Search for your child's profile even if you and your child are not friends (yet). You can use the information below to evaluate their profile:

- ✓ Is their profile public? By this we mean, if you click on your child's name, it should say "Suzie only shares certain information with everyone. If you know Suzie, add her as a friend on Facebook."
- ✓ Can you see some of their friends? You may or may not think it is appropriate for outsiders to see who is on your child's friend list, especially because a user can click on the friend's name and then go to their profile.
- ✓ What other information comes up? Does their school name or city? You can decide what you think is best for your child and help them adjust their privacy settings accordingly.

One of our partners was shocked to see that her nephew, who is only 14, listed his high school on his public searchable profile so if someone is searching and finds him, they know where he attends school. Another partner found that her 12 year-old nephew listed his complete home phone number and middle school! Even though he isn't allowed by Facebook to have a profile, he had misrepresented his birth date in order to be on Facebook. That was a little disturbing to say the least.

Chapter 11: Creating Friend List

Facebook offers a great way to organize your friends into various groups. For example, you can create a list that contains your family members, another list for your friends from a book club, a list that has business contacts, yet another one that has all your friends from a particular networking group. The added advantage of creating lists is that each list can be assigned different privacy setting. Remember that a friend's privacy setting will always default to the most restrictive list you add them to.

A couple of notes about friend lists:

- ✓ You can place any friend into multiple Friend Lists.
- ✓ You can have unlimited number of Friend Lists.
- ✓ Each Friend List can have a different privacy setting.

Creating Friend Lists:

Go to "Account," click on "Edit Friends," locate "Friends" link in the left menu (under "Lists") and click on it. This will bring the listing of all your Facebook friends.

You will be able to create a new Friend List by clicking on the "Create New List" link.

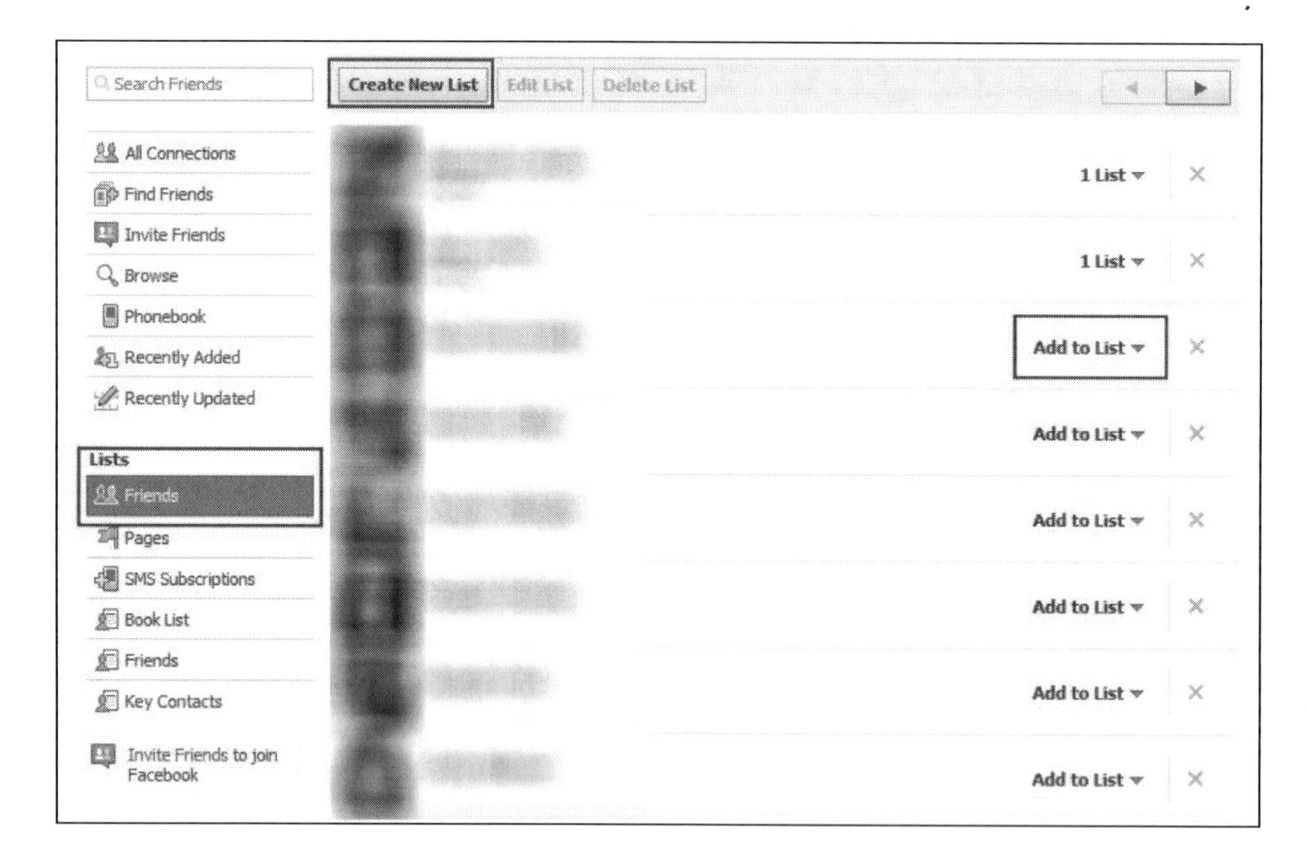

When you click on the "Create New List" link, a window will pop up asking you to name your list. The search box in the upper right allows you to search through your friends to find the people you want to add to the list.

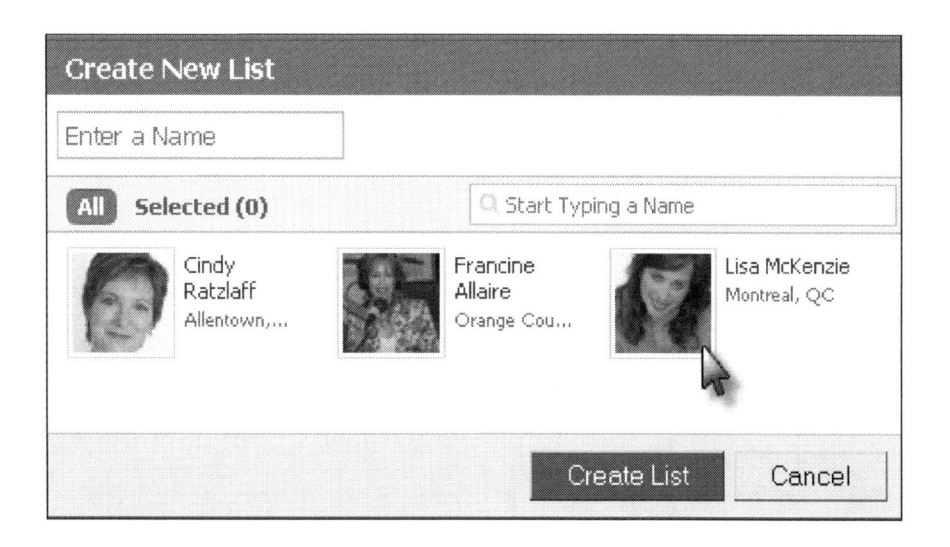

Clicking on a friend's name or picture will add them to the list, and their entry will now have a blue box with a checkmark around it to indicate that they have been selected as members of this list.

As you can see we've named our list "Key Contacts" and selected Lisa and Cindy to be a part of the list. When you've selected all the friends for your list, click the Create List button to complete the process. This List is now added to your "Lists."

Now, when you click on "Key Contacts," only friends that you added to this list will be shown.

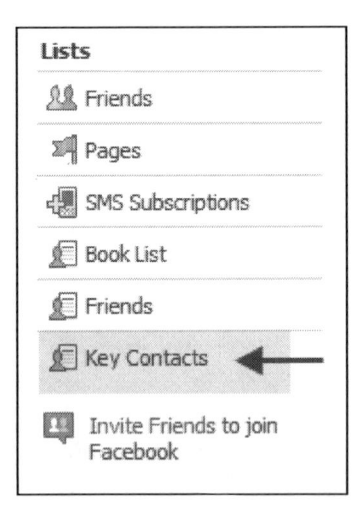

Using Friend Lists:

You can create as many friend lists as you wish.

Once a list is selected, you will only see the updates from the people in that list in the in the newsfeed area.

For example, you could create a list for co-workers, family, close friends, associates from a club or organization and so on — and any time you wanted to check in with that group, you could do so very easily from your Home page without having to sort through lots of other posts.

The other way to use the lists is in setting your profile privacy settings. Remember the "customize" option when setting up your privacy settings?

You can see here that "specific people" allows you to enter a "name or a LIST"

You can even use friend lists when you do status updates. On the "what's on your mind" area, there is a little "lock."

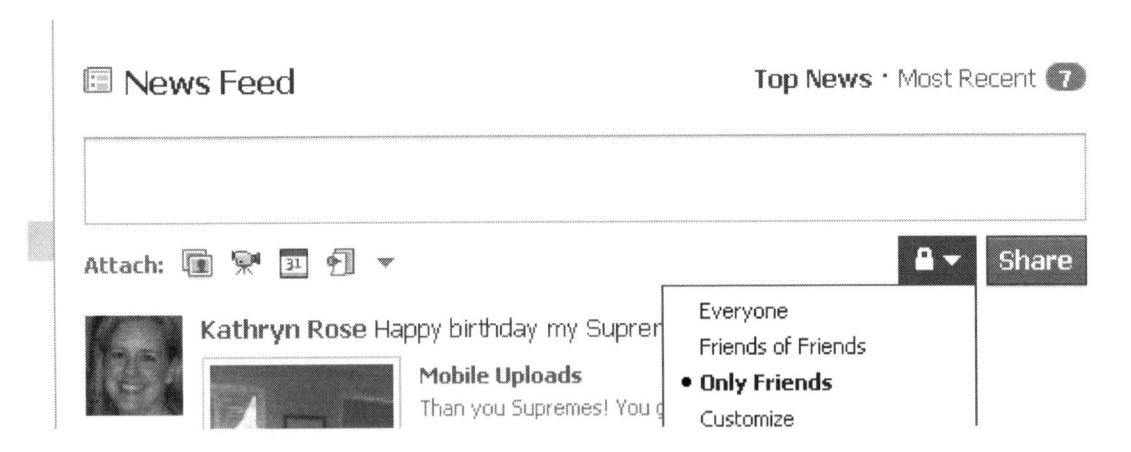

From here you click "customize" and then "specific people" and send your status update to only the folks on that list.

Chapter 12: To Friend or Not to Friend, That is the Question

So many kids think that they have to amass hundreds, even thousands of friends to be popular on Facebook which in their mind transcends to popularity in real life. Hey, we probably would have thought the same thing at their age. But online you have to protect your information. As you saw in the privacy settings, if you're not careful about who you "friend," you could be giving away a whole lot of information you wouldn't normally give out in person. Let's face it. Would you give a stranger your address, phone number, vacation schedule or pictures of you or your kids? We think not.

You might not suspect that someone who doesn't know you or your child at all would even want to friend them, but it happens all the time. We get friend requests from total strangers every day.

You may want to "friend" a parent of another child in your son/daughters group just to connect. When we were growing up, all the moms in the neighborhood kept an eye on us when we were outside. Now we need to do the same thing for one another's children when they're outside in cyberspace.

Friending people:

When you receive a friend request from someone you don't know, the first thing you should look for is a personal note. It is very important if someone is requesting to be your friend that they tell you who they are and why they are asking to be your friend. It's not enough that they say, Suzie Miller suggested we become friends because as you saw before, they could have gotten Suzie's name from a simple Facebook search. Also looking at any friends in common could perhaps indicate where the connection could stem.

Then EVEN IF YOU KNOW THEM, take a look at their profile. Is it public? How do you know them? It is not enough to simply look and see "ohh, we have friends in common." Many children see that they have friends in common and think it's ok to accept the request. They should never accept a friend request from someone they do not know. And as adult, be aware that many of your friends may be using Facebook for business and accepting friend requests from total strangers. So it's not a good idea to use "friends in common" as your sole reason for accepting a friend request. Do your homework just as you would before inviting someone into your home.

From there you can either ignore the request or accept it. If you chose to ignore a request, don't worry. People are not notified when their friend requests are ignored.

If you choose to accept someone as a friend, check out their profile and their wall and make sure their content is appropriate. One of our members, who we like to call "the Facebook police," checks any of her kids' friends profiles to see if they put their birth date or give away other information she thinks should remain private, and then sends a direct message

(note: not a Wall post) to the child letting them know that they should think about changing some of their privacy settings for safety reasons.

Un-friending people:

If someone you "friended" turns out to post inappropriate things or just posts sales message after sales message to attempt to entice you to buy something, you can easily "unfriend" them.

Go to the blue navigation bar across the top and click "Edit Friends."

In the left menu bar section click on either "All Connections" or below in the "Lists" section "Friends." This will pull up all your friends where you can make a choice on "unfriending" them by clicking on the "X" to the right "Remove Connection" and confirm it.

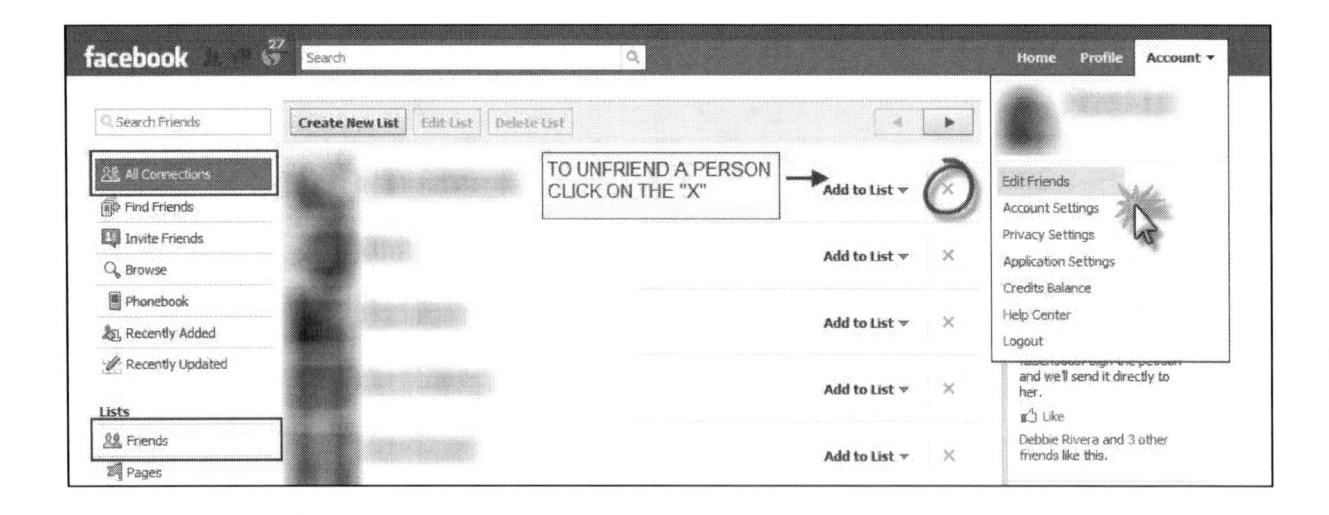

Don't worry. The person will not be notified. But, if they go to their own friend list or try and click on your profile, they will notice that you are either missing or they cannot access your profile.

Facebook® Guide for Parents 98

© SupremeSocialMedia.com

Chapter 13: Friends Options Review

Let's review our friends options. Click on "Account" and "Edit Friends." Options on this page are:

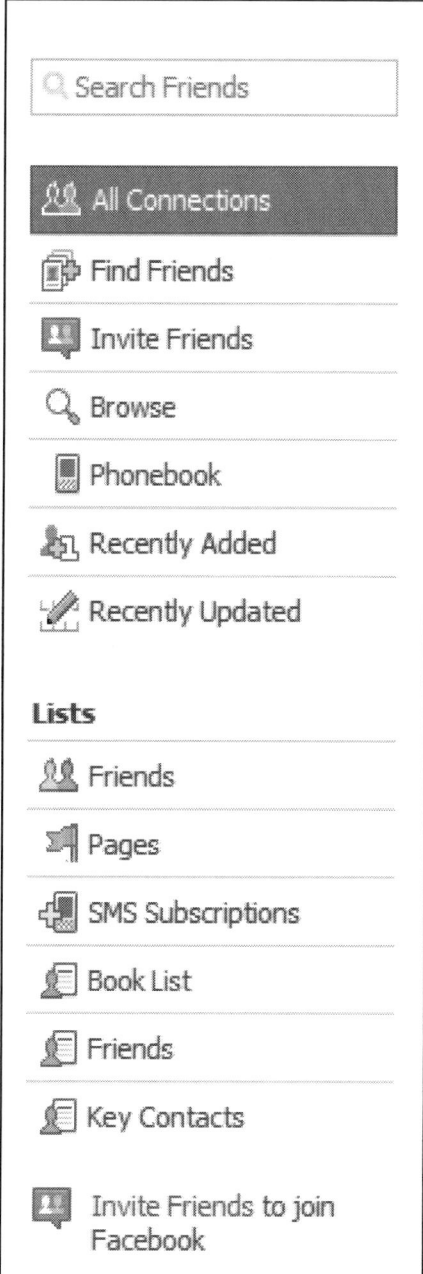

1. Search Friends: start typing the name of your Facebook friend here and the list of friends will appear. From here, you click on the Friend's picture to go to their Wall/Profile page.

2. All Connections: alphabetical list of all your Facebook connections, including friends, groups and pages.

3. Find Friends: find people you may know from your email and IM contacts, your Facebook networks (high school classmates, college alumni, or past or current co-workers).

Facebook® Guide for Parents 99

© SupremeSocialMedia.com

4. Invite Friends: create an "in" Facebook email and send a message to your email contacts inviting them to join you on Facebook.

5. Browse: search existing Facebook friends by College, High School, Work or City.

6. Phonebook: alphabetical list of your Facebook friends that have listed their phone contact information.

7. Recently Added: list of your latest Facebook friends.

8. Recently Updated: listing of all friends that made changes or updates to their Facebook account.

Facebook® Guide for Parents 100

© SupremeSocialMedia.com

Lists Options:

1. Friends: alphabetical listing of all your Facebook friends.

2. Pages: alphabetical listing of all Pages you "Liked."

3. SMS Subscriptions: subscribe to receiving mobile text updates every time your friends' update their status. Caution: text message charges apply and depend on your mobile account setup.

4. Book List, Friends and Key Contacts are the PRIVATE Lists created and named by the user.

Chapter 14: Creating User Name Link

Facebook allows users to choose a unique username. Users are now able to direct others to their profile page through a simple link such as http://Facebook.com/yourname

> http://www.facebook.com/katrose

instead of a long and complex URL like this one:

> http://www.facebook.com/profile.php?id=14836009468&ref=nf

Usernames are available to any existing or newly registered user. Before you can create your user name URL, Facebook will ask you to verify your account via mobile phone. This is not complicated at all if you follow the instructions on the screen and does not link your page to your mobile phone or turn on Facebook mobile messaging. It is simply a way to verify that you're real.

To set up your Unique User Name URL, you must first Login to your account. Then click on this link and follow directions.
http://facebook.com/username
YOU MUST BE LOGGED IN TO YOUR ACCOUNT BEFORE GOING TO THIS LINK.

Chapter 15: Removing Posts

OOPS! I messed up and posted something on my wall that I didn't mean to put there. Can I remove it? Yes!

How to remove posts once they are live:

Simply go to your wall, hover your mouse below the "Options" button on the upper right corner of the post and a "Remove" button will appear. Click "Remove" on the box next to the post. A box will come up asking if you're sure you want to delete. You can delete your posts, as well as others who may have posted on your wall.

> **Susan Miller** What a beautiful night in the northeast!
> about a minute ago · Comment · Like
>
> Options
> Remove

This removes the post from your wall and any of your friends' news feeds where it might have been posted.

Chapter 16: Reputation Monitoring

As parents, we understand how important it is to protect our children's (and our own) reputation online. Once something is out there, it's out there forever. So how do you find it once it's posted?

FREE SITES

Google Alerts is a great free tool that emails you automatically when there are new Google results for your search terms. You can set up a Google alert for your name, your child's name or any subject where you want regular alerts. Google currently offers alerts with results from News, Web, Blogs, Video and Groups.

According to the Google Alerts website, you can sign up for 6 variations of alerts: 'News," "Web," "Blogs," "Comprehensive," "Video" and "Groups."

News alert - an email aggregate of the latest news articles that contain the search terms of your choice and appear in the top ten results of your Google News search.

Web alert - an email aggregate of the latest web pages that contain the search terms of your choice and appear in the top twenty results of your Google Web search.

Blogs alert - an email aggregate of the latest blog posts that contain the search terms of your choice and appear in the top ten results of your Google Blog search.

Comprehensive alert - an aggregate of the latest results from multiple sources (News, Web and Blogs) into a single email to provide maximum coverage on the topic of your choice.

Video alert - an email aggregate of the latest videos that contain the search terms of your choice and appear in the top ten results of your Google Video search.

Groups alert - an email aggregate of new posts that contain the search terms of your choice and appear in the top fifty results of your Google Groups search.

We recommend when you set up alerts, you make sure to use all variations of your name and your child's name including nicknames. The best way to set up the alerts is in **quotes**. For example "Your Name" this way you will get only alerts that include both of the words YOUR and NAME as one phrase.

Otherwise, you could end up receiving alerts on any time someone mentions YOUR or NAME. In Susan Miller's case, she'd get notified every time someone mentioned the name Susan or the name Miller. That could be overwhelming and not useful.

How to set up Google Alerts:

Go to http://www.google.com/alerts

You can set this up so alerts are sent to your own email or set it up through a GMAIL account. You can set up multiple alerts for the same name across different categories if you like.

PAID SITES

There are many sites on the internet now to help you monitor your reputation. "Reputation Defender" is one of the sites we have found that does this for a fee and is much more in depth than Google Alerts.

Find it at http://www.reputationdefender.com

Search Facebook

You can also search Facebook to see if someone is referencing your child. To do this go to the search bar, type your child's name in, in quotes. Hit enter then when the page comes up make sure you go to the bottom and click "posts by everyone." This will bring up a search in real time of people talking about anyone with your child's name.

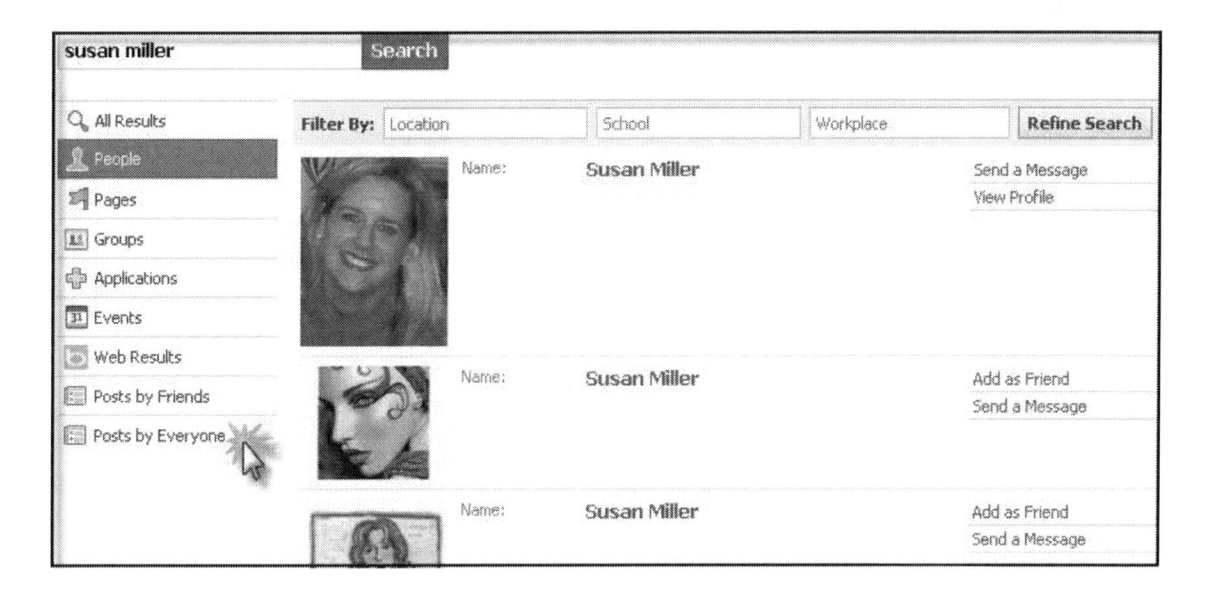

Chapter 17: HELP- My Ungrateful Child "Unfriended" Me!

This is every parent's nightmare! The truth is, folks, unless you set up their account and hold onto the password, (which is what we recommend for younger children) the simple fact is there is no way to force your child to "friend" you. Think of it as the diary of our day. Did you show your parents your diary? We consider it a privilege if our older kids let us in and keep us in the loop. Younger kids are a different story. We believe parents should exercise strong parental control over those accounts while giving kids enough freedom to learn appropriate online etiquette and safety measures.

We can, however, offer some tips on what you can do or not do to up your chances of staying on your child's "friend" list (all examples from http://myparentsjoinedfacebook.com):

Don't write embarrassing things on your CHILD's wall.

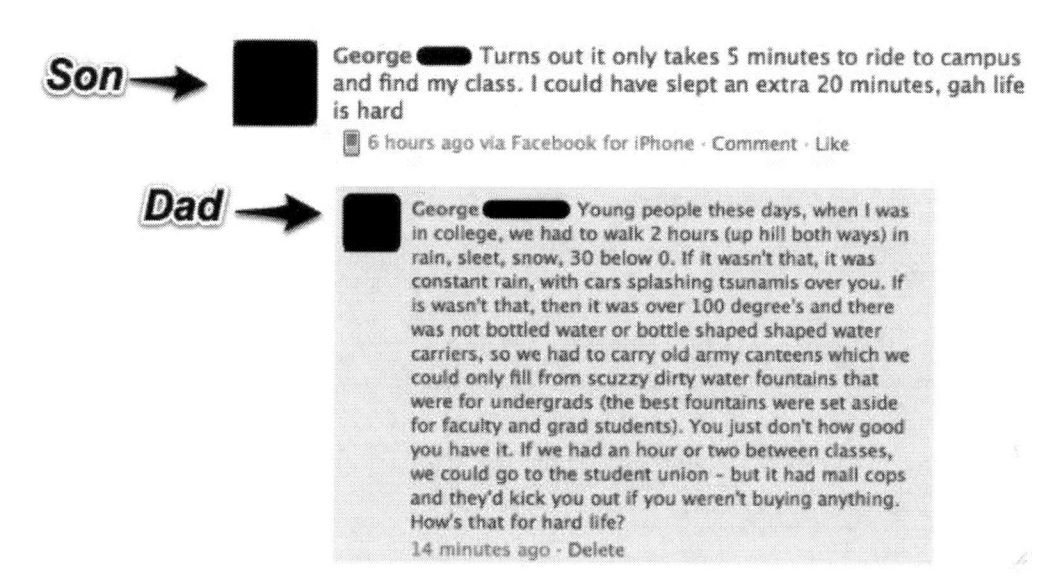

Son → George ■ Turns out it only takes 5 minutes to ride to campus and find my class. I could have slept an extra 20 minutes, gah life is hard
6 hours ago via Facebook for iPhone · Comment · Like

Dad → George ■ Young people these days, when I was in college, we had to walk 2 hours (up hill both ways) in rain, sleet, snow, 30 below 0. If it wasn't that, it was constant rain, with cars splashing tsunamis over you. If is wasn't that, then it was over 100 degree's and there was not bottled water or bottle shaped shaped water carriers, so we had to carry old army canteens which we could only fill from scuzzy dirty water fountains that were for undergrads (the best fountains were set aside for faculty and grad students). You just don't how good you have it. If we had an hour or two between classes, we could go to the student union - but it had mall cops and they'd kick you out if you weren't buying anything. How's that for hard life?
14 minutes ago · Delete

Don't write embarrassing things on YOUR wall that could end up in your child's news feed and most likely on to their friends' news feeds.

■ ▇▇▇▇ Hot and sticky this afternoon...But had a fun morning with my husband......If you know what I mean..Ha ha
14 minutes ago ▢ Comment ▢ Like

▇▇▇▇ MOTHER!
about a minute ago ▢ Delete

Write a comment...

Don't freak out over every little post: pick your battles.

> **Michael** ▇▇▇▇ I blew one hard last night
> Posted about an hour ago · Comment · Like
>
> > **Charlene** ▇▇▇▇ at 2:58pm April 5
> > What's that mean Michael? MOM

Don't panic if they "unfriend" you. Try and find out why they did it. Then, sit down and discuss the privacy settings with them. If YOU can't see what is going on, they should make sure NO ONE else outside of their friends can see either. Use this as an opportunity to start a discussion. Often your child will "friend" you again after a good discussion about boundaries and communication. This is a potential teaching moment and worth the discomfort.

If your younger child won't friend you, at the very least you should insist on seeing their "Info" page occasionally to make sure they haven't exposed too much personal information. It is VERY likely that your child will friend someone they don't know very well, if at all. At least this way that person won't have access to your home address and phone number.

Facebook® Guide for Parents 110

© SupremeSocialMedia.com

As we mentioned in the beginning of the book, we are not child psychologists. We are mothers, daughters, sisters and aunts speaking from our own personal and mostly professional experience. So here is our personal advice on speaking to your children.

Kathryn Rose: *Facebook is such a great way to connect with people but it also can be a little scary. Kids can get in some trouble accepting friend requests from people who may not be so friendly. My mother (yes, she was passive aggressive HA HA) used to leave the "Dear Abby" section folded up by my breakfast bowl if there was an article she thought might get a point across. If you just leave this book around, your child might pick it up, just to find out what you know. The other thing my parents would do is ask for my "help" in setting up something and this would open up the conversation.*

Just like when we were teenagers, we can't force our children to allow us to participate in their online world. You just have to have an open dialog with them at all times about what is going on and hopefully that will help direct them

For younger children, I suggest you set up the account and control the password. This way they cannot access Facebook without you being there. If they have a profile outside of your control make them take it down.

For older children, make sure you pick your battles. Maybe you don't ask them about every single post they make. Or, if their friends say something inappropriate, don't get on your child's case about it. The main thing is to make sure they are protected and don't post or say anything that could come back to bite them later. This includes "Mrs. Smith gave us a tough test today, she's such a meanie." That is mild, but there is a chance it could get back to Mrs. Smith. She may see it herself, or a child who is upset with your child may tell her. Explain to your child the consequences of posting things they wouldn't say to someone in person. Either way, it's best to not say anything online that you don't want to come back at you.

Where it gets tougher is when you see posts from your child's FRIENDS that worry you and you wonder how to handle it. Personally, I might try and talk to the other child instead of going right to their parents unless it is something pretty severe. I would definitely let my child know I saw it and have to take some action. If I thought the child was in real danger, I would consider contacting the parent.

In the case of cyber-bullying however, time is of the essence. All of us can remember the sting of another child's words. Think of it as the "bathroom wall" writing of our day, except now it's plastered all over the internet for the world to see—years and years from now. Make sure your child knows they can come to you and tell you if they are being bullied and make sure they understand that it is totally unacceptable for them to bully others.

Cindy Ratzlaff: *Here's my rule with younger teens. You must simply insist that if they want to have a Facebook profile, they have to friend you. Strike a bargain with your child that you won't comment (very often) on their wall. Be very clear with them that you're there because you are responsible for their safety and you need to be able to check in on them and the people they talk to on line. Go over the rules with them. Let them know you're reading what's on their wall. Make sure they are clear that bad language, bullying, and threats are unacceptable to you and that you will shut them down if they disobey these strict rules. Once all that is established, they'll still forget that you're watching because they're kids. You know what it's like when you drive a gang of kids to a soccer game and they talk amongst themselves as though you're not in the car? That's what happens on Facebook. You'll be able to observe relationships and interactions, "hear" what's going on at school, learn how your child interacts with peers and discover how they view the world around them. You can always step in if there are real problems. But mostly, you'll be sitting ringside in their world.*

Once you have older teens, a lot of the same issues take place but they may not always listen to you and they may, indeed, unfriend you if your presence is too obvious. My college daughter and I are Facebook friends, but I know better than to post on her wall. If I see something that makes me long to ask a question, I e-mail her. Because Facebook is a public platform, I'd never ask a deeply personal or private question, even in the "Wall-to-Wall" which I learned the hard way, is not private. Because I'm respectful of her space, she still allows me to peek in now and then.

And because I do, we've had some wonderfully deep conversations about her college experience that might otherwise not have come to pass.

Lisa McKenzie: *We have two younger children who often ask what Facebook is all about. They are also witnessing their older friends strong attempts to convince their parents to allow them to join, especially now with all the fun games only accessible through Facebook. They watch how older kids and adults post funny comments, pictures and videos and want in on the excitement. My husband and I are strong mobile users so Facebook is accessible any and everywhere from our iPhone, even a doctor's waiting room can be made fun. If I was a child, you bet I would want to virtually hang out with my friends, laugh and read all kinds of cool stuff.*

The key is to involve your children in the fun of Facebook so they don't feel left out. The minimum age for kids to sign up for Facebook is 13 years old, of course younger kids sign up all the time with or without their parents permission. If your child is on Facebook, you need to know to protect their identity and ensure their privacy settings are set correctly. Take the time to explain to your children that when they post a comment or a picture on Facebook that they take everyone's best interest into consideration and don't share private matters that may offend or hurt someone's feelings. This early understanding of privacy is important to their education of using online tools from Facebook to even simple emails. Keeping the conversation light and amusing is what keeps Facebook fun.

Francine Allaire: *Put your best face forward. I'm of the opinion that "social" doesn't mean "personal." Too many people are making the mistakes of sharing way too much information and they fail to remember that the digital footprint is forever. Learn about Social Media so you can engage and even teach your children some online etiquette. I would like to offer the following tips: 1. Never say anything via email or on social networking sites you wouldn't say publicly about or to someone face-to-face. 2. Don't write or share anything you wouldn't want your mother or your child to see. Once you put it on Facebook, even if you remove it later, it is likely to be something that can haunt you. If your mother, grandmother, kids, spouse or a current or future boss or client shouldn't see it, DON'T post it.*

We are now living in the communication age. The social networks provide a venue in which people can connect and communicate with each other, like virtual neighborhoods. And in our ever-flattening and highly technological world, this venue is likely to continue to grow and evolve over time. Bottom line – it's not going away anytime soon. So get engaged and talk to your children openly about their use of these exciting tools. And most of all, relax have some fun with it too.

Chapter 18: Joining and Starting Groups

You can start connecting with people by using your personal contacts as well as finding new people who have similar interest through Facebook Groups. The easiest way to search for a group is by typing in the search bar on the blue navigation area. Try something like your child's school.

I typed in "Main Street School" and got these results:

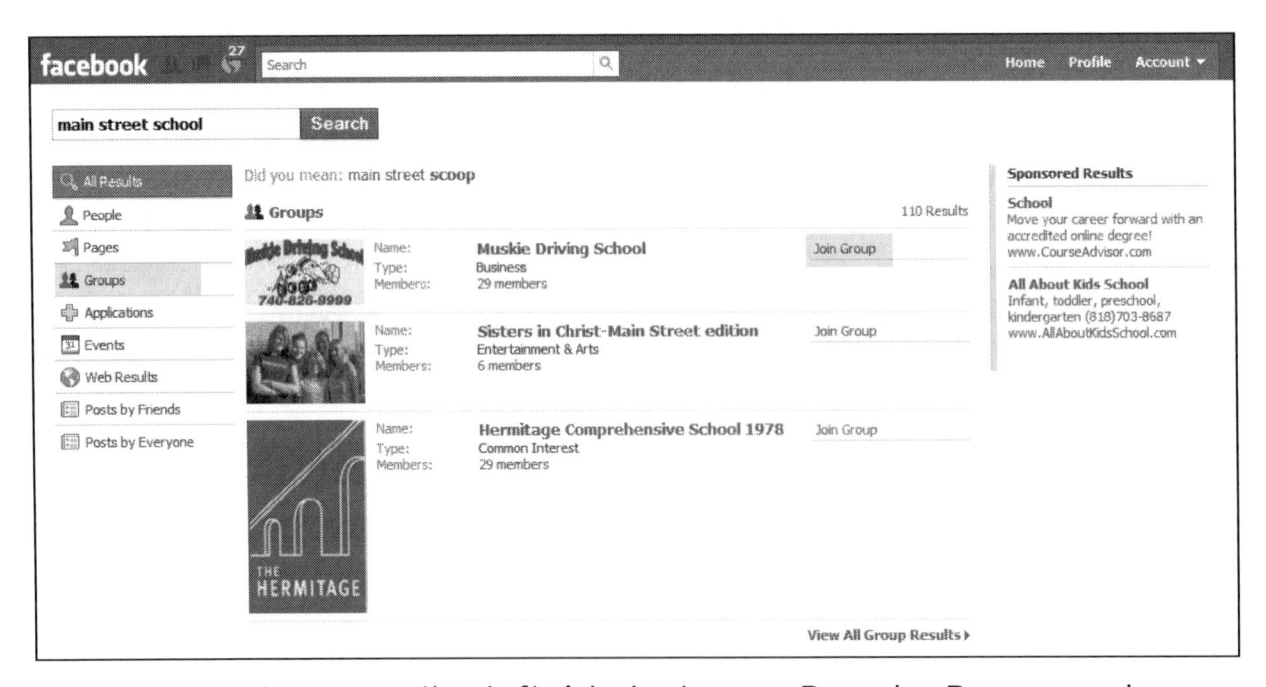

You can sort now on the left side between People, Pages and Groups to find your school and see if there is a parents' group or PTA of some kind. If not, you can always start your own group.

Creating a group on Facebook

To create a Facebook Group, go to the "Groups" icon located in the left menu bar of your "Home" page.

From here, you can search for groups and also create a new group. For example, you can create a parents group for your child's school so you can connect with other parents.

To create your own group, click on "Groups" and "+ Create a Group."

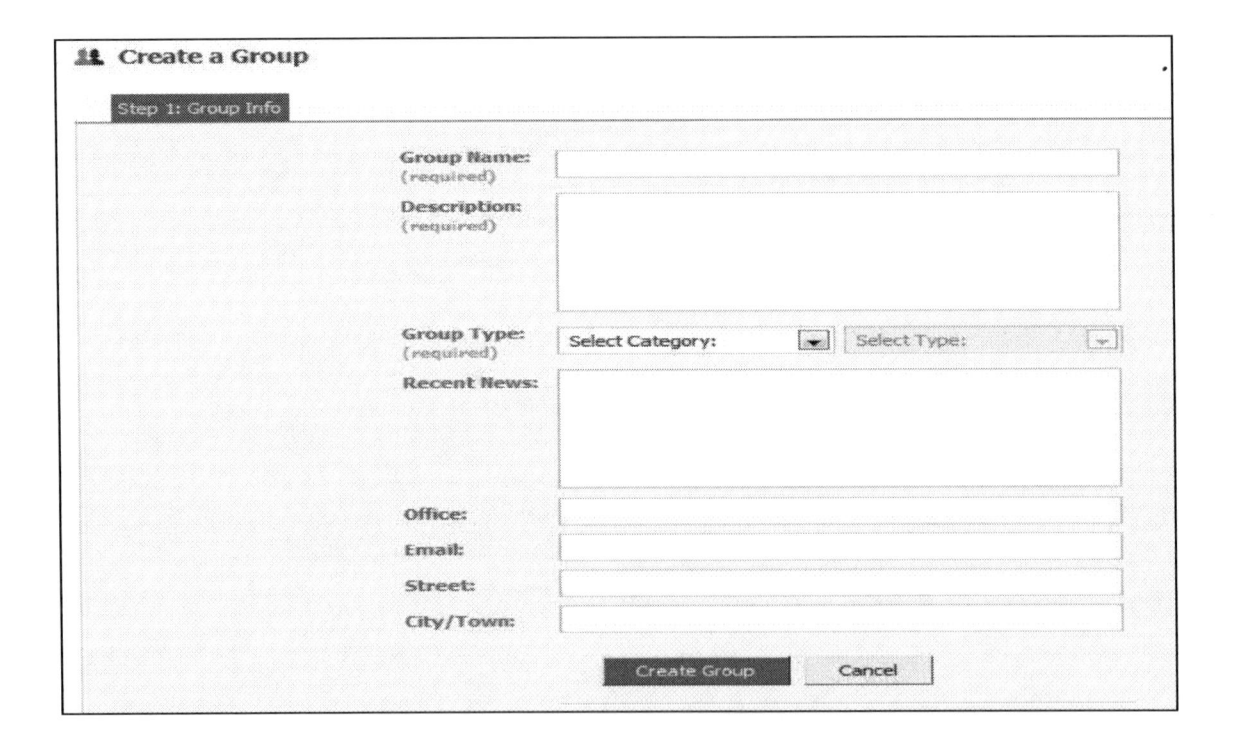

Fill out all required fields and any others that may be important to the group members. Always keep in mind who will have access to the details and keep your personal information to a minimum. The next screen will take you through a series of choices you will carefully consider in order to customize it. Here is where you can make the group private or public, among other choices.

Facebook® Guide for Parents 118

© SupremeSocialMedia.com

Once you click on the "Save" button, Facebook will ask you if you want to PUBLISH to your wall. At this time SKIP this and publish it LATER. The next step is to invite friends to become members.

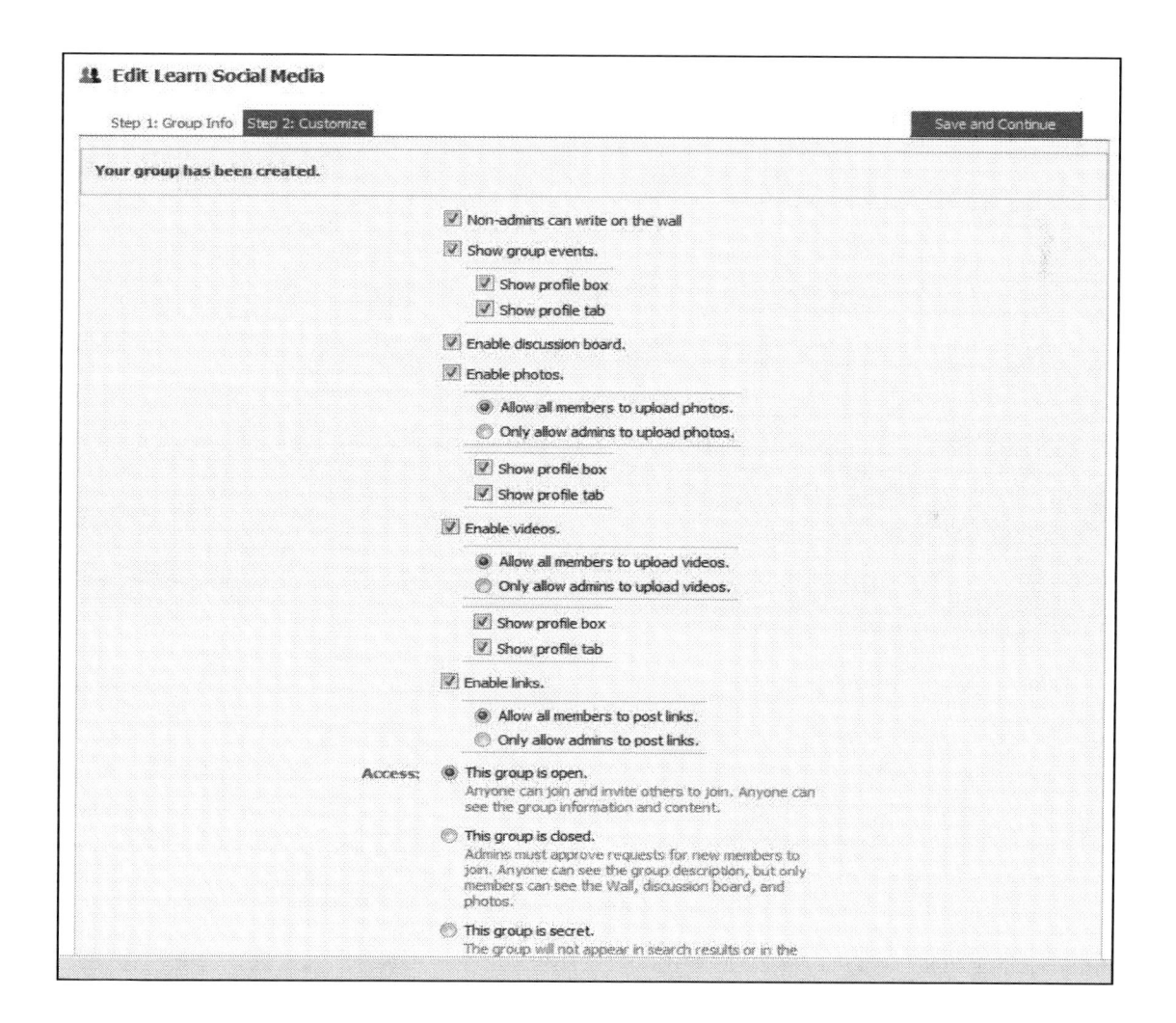

You have couple of choices here. You can invite your friends by clicking on their picture/name, or you can insert email addresses.

Make sure to add a personal message in which you will tell them a bit about your group and why it will benefit them to join.

When you click on "Back to (your group name)" link in the upper right corner, you will land on the INFO page of your group, which you can always edit by clicking in Edit Information link.

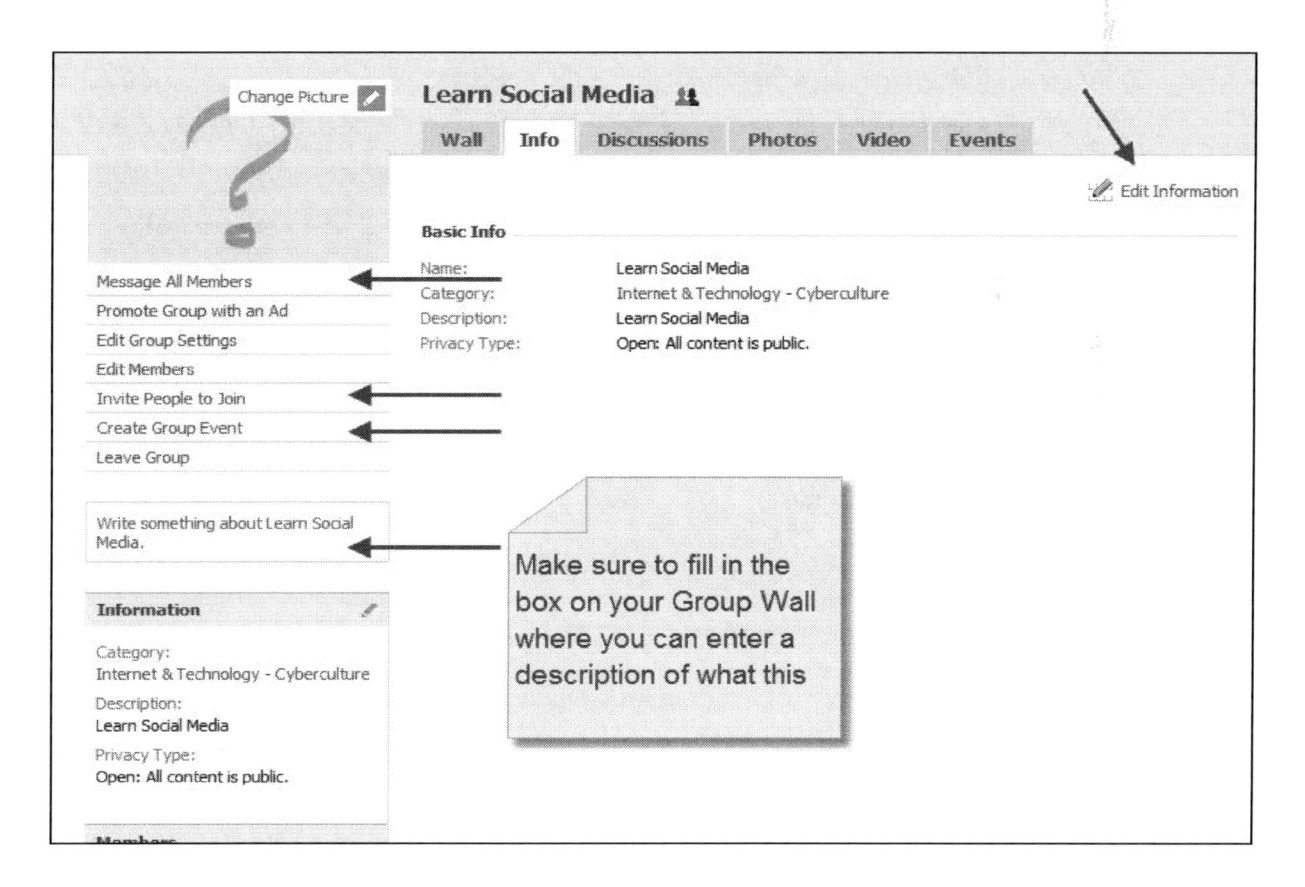

Make sure to fill in the box on your Group Wall where you can enter a description of what this

Chapter 19: Uploading Photos and Videos

One of the most popular applications on Facebook is the Photos application. The main features of this application are:

- Upload unlimited numbers of photos.
- Create photo albums.
- Post comments on your friends' photos and albums.
- Privacy settings for individual <u>albums</u>, limiting the groups of users that can see an album. For example, the privacy of an album can be set so that only the user's friends can see the album, while the privacy of another album can be set so that all Facebook users can see it.

According to Facebook there are:

- 1.7 billion user photos uploaded to their servers
- 2.2 billion friends tagged in user photos
- 60+ million photos added each week to Facebook servers
- 3+ billion photo images served to users every day
- 100,000+ images served per second during peak traffic windows

One of the most fun things you can do with Facebook is share photos and videos. There are a couple of different ways to upload photos and videos. The process is the same for both (photos AND videos).

To do a quick photo post, go to your status update box put in a status update and then click on either photo or video in the "attach" area. You'll be prompted to upload and it's that easy.

The other way to share photos is to create a photo album

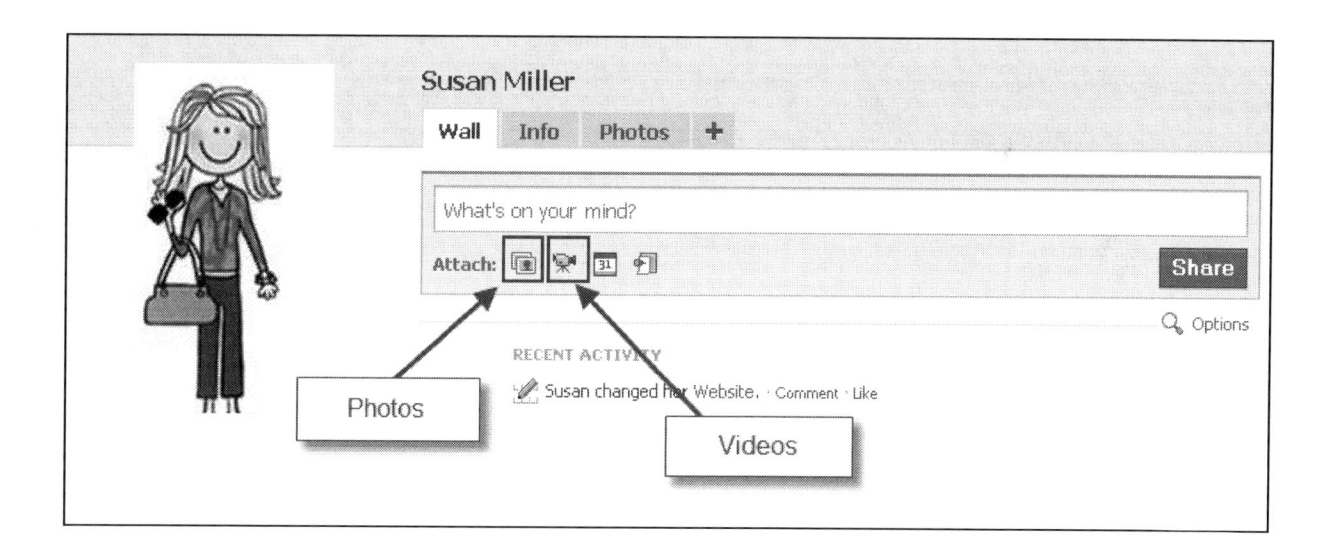

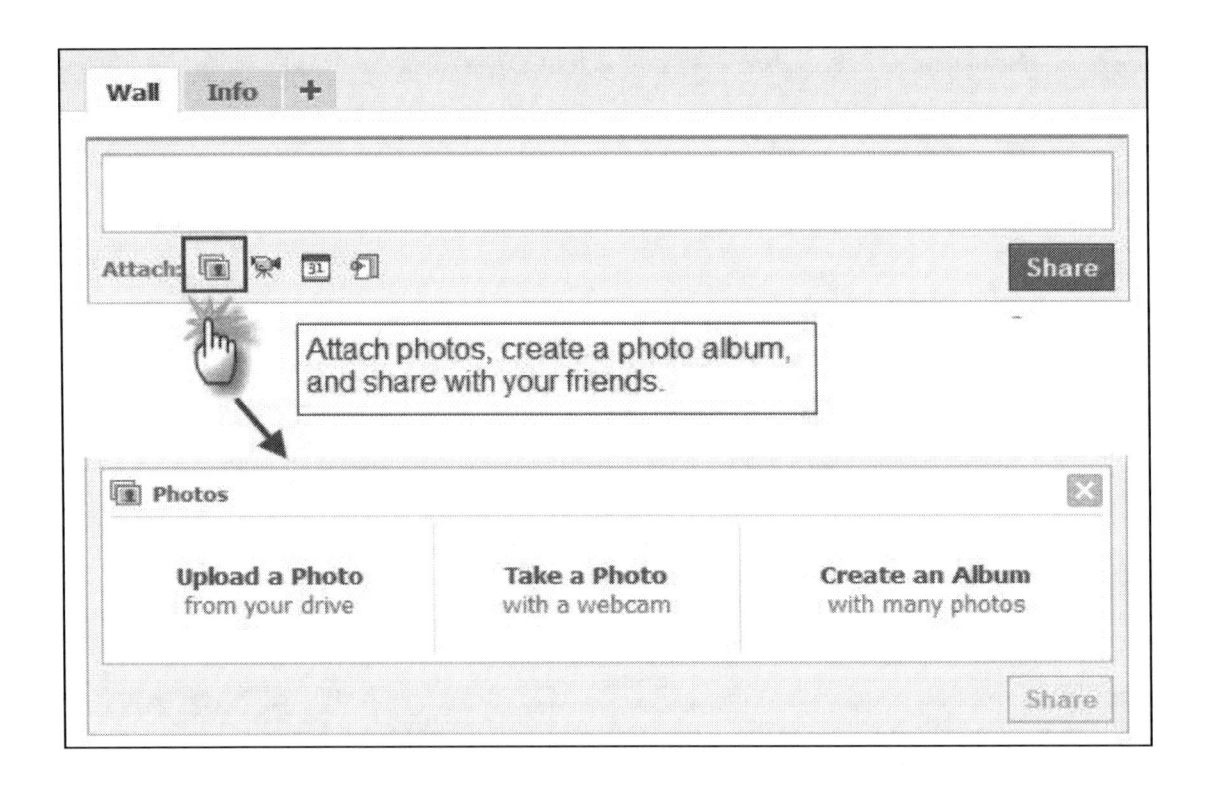

You can find Photos by clicking on the "Photos" link in the left menu bar of the "Home" page. Click on "My uploads." You will see that each photo is tagged by its name.

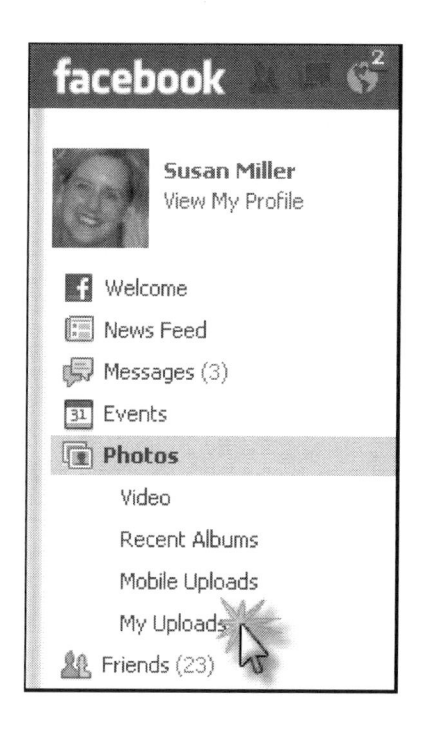

If you uploaded an album, there is an option to "Edit Album" located underneath the photo/album name. This is where you can adjust "Edit Info" and then you'll be taken to a screen where you can make privacy adjustments (photo below).

Facebook® Guide for Parents 125

© SupremeSocialMedia.com

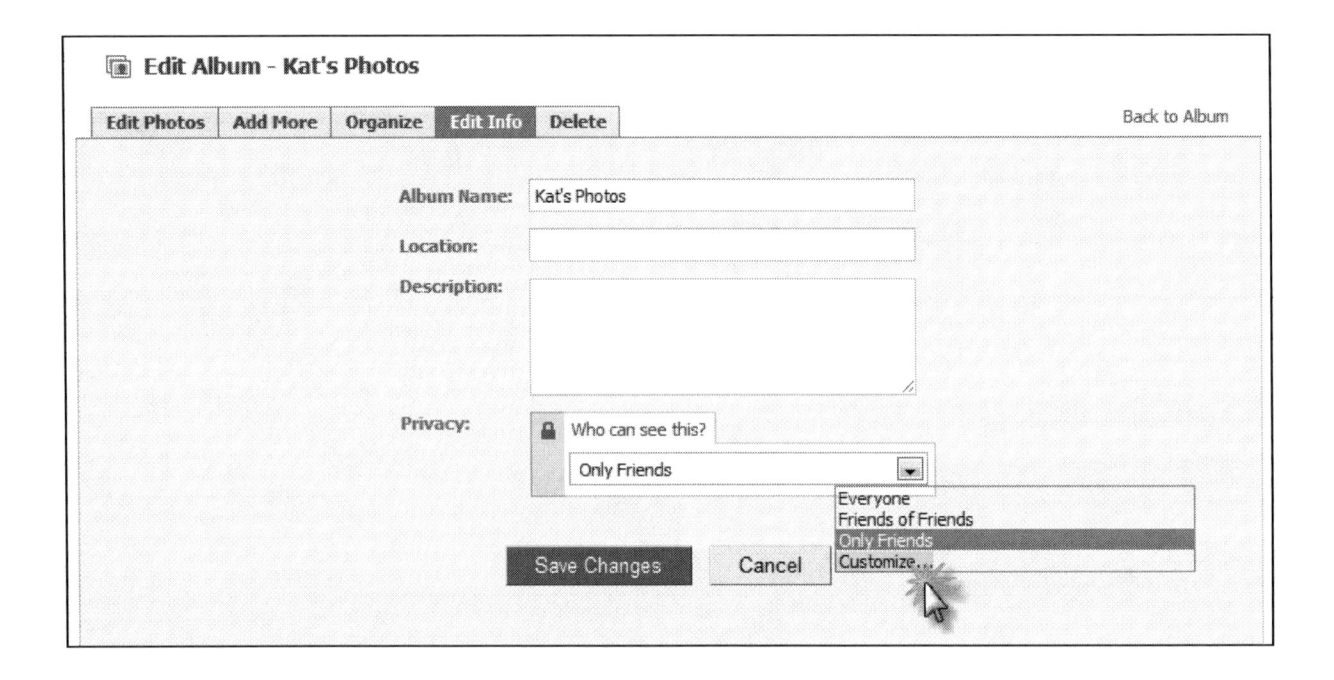

Here, you can add or change the name of your album, create a brief description and decide who can and cannot see your album. If these are pictures of your children, you may want to set the album at "Only friends" under the privacy settings drop down menu. Under location, you can add additional information about the album or just leave it blank.

As with all privacy settings on Facebook, you can "customize" privacy settings for your photos or entire albums. Here is the screen shot of the all options Facebook has created to give you the complete power of the decision of who can or can't view your photos.

Tagging Photos of People:

As we mentioned in a previous chapter, Facebook offers users the ability to "tag" or label users in a photo. For instance, if a photo contains a user's friend, then the user can tag the friend in the photo. This sends a notification to the friend that they have been tagged, and provides them a link to see the photo.

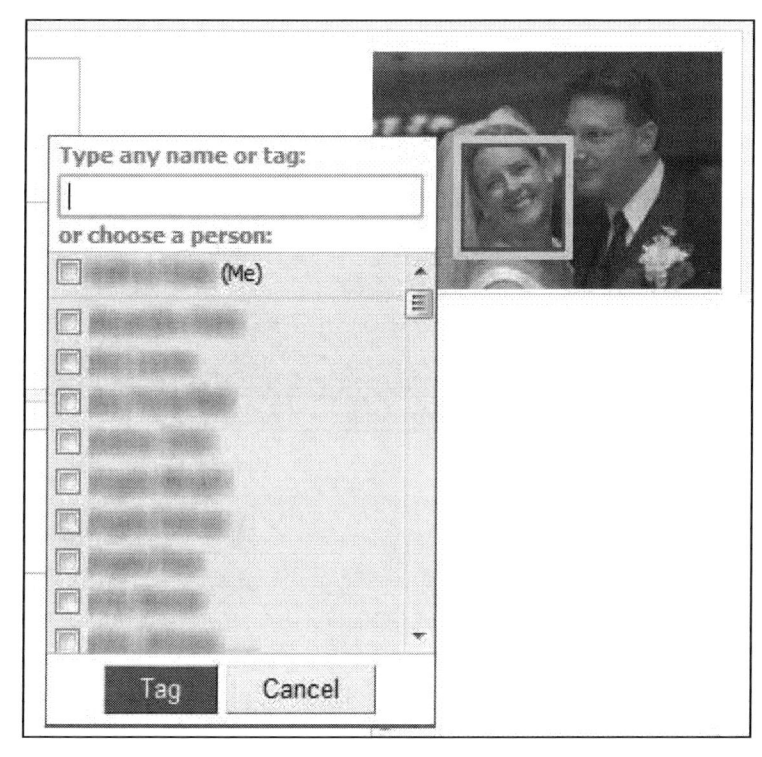

To "tag" someone in a photo, just click on their face – the square will appear framing your friend's face and another drop-down menu will allow you to start typing your friend's name, choose from the list by clicking on the name. When your friends are tagged in your photo, they will receive the notification that they have been tagged in a photo including the link to the photo they have been tagged in. They will have the option to "remove tag" if they want to.

Once you are done uploading the pictures, tags and description, at the bottom of the page you'll see a "Save Changes" button. Click that button, go to the top of your page and click "Publish Now" if you're ready. You can also choose to skip that step and not publish right now. Your album will be saved and you can publish it later.

Once you click "publish" your photos go out into your News Feed and are published to your profile. You can view them on your own profile by clicking on the "photos" tab or clicking on the "photos of me" under your picture (see image on the next page):

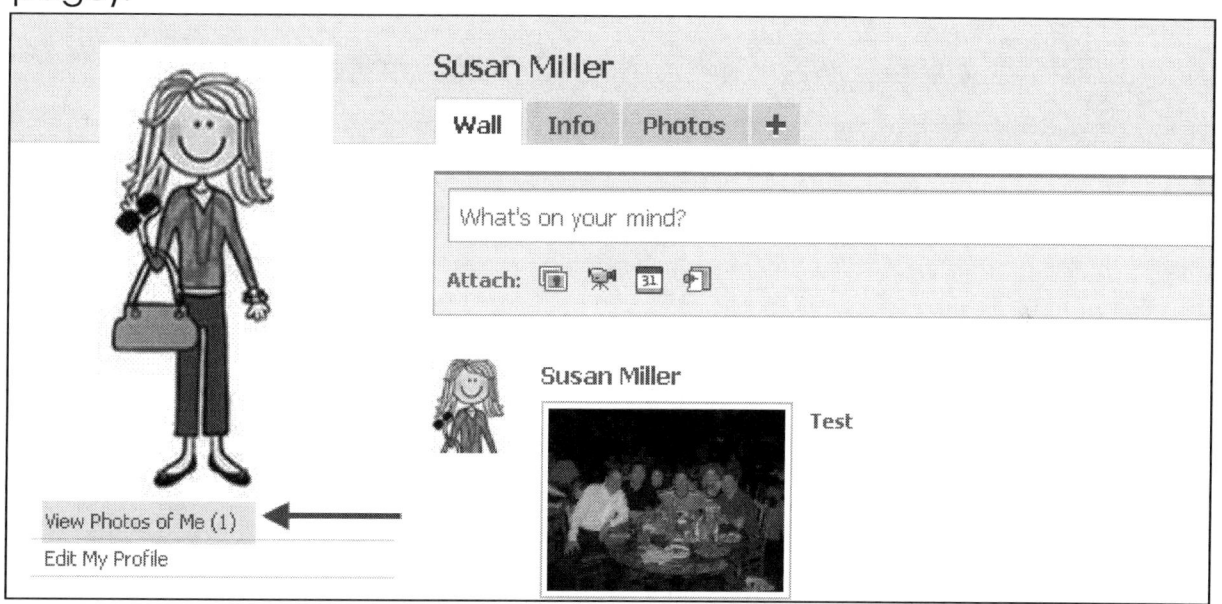

Sharing Your Photos:

You can share this album with your friends even if they are not on Facebook by clicking the "Share This Album with Friends even if they are not on Facebook" link.

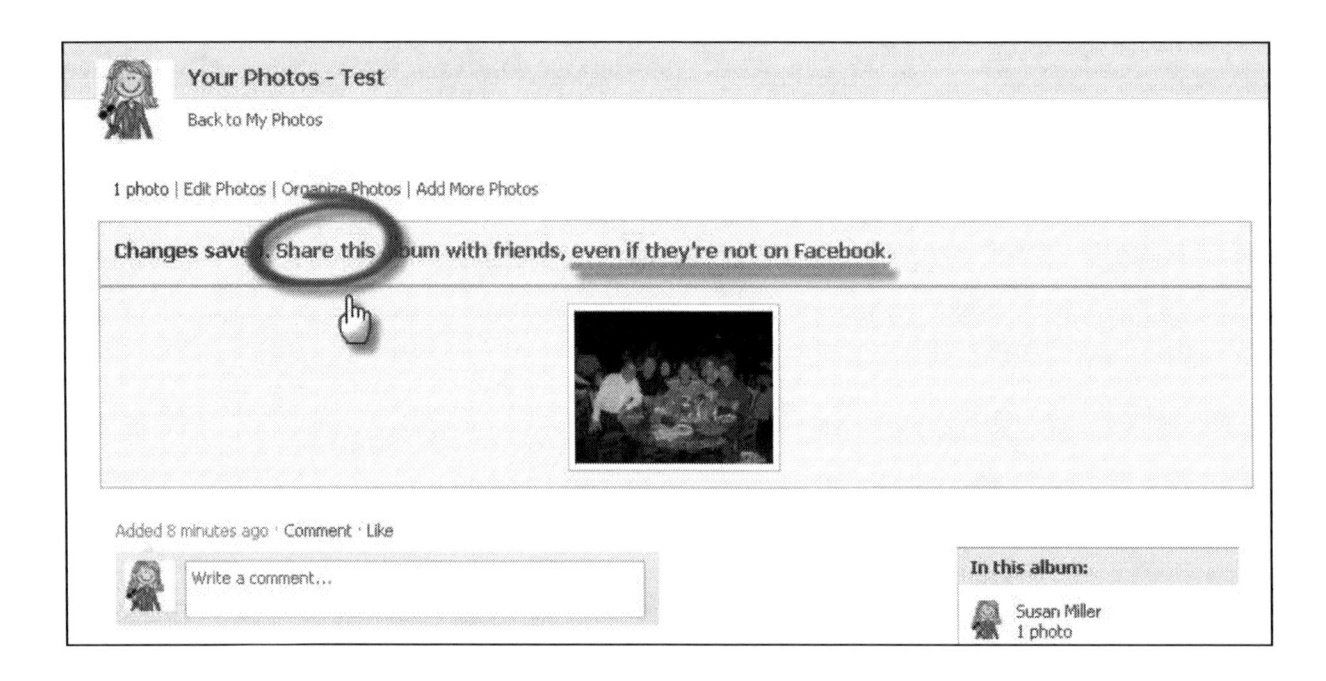

Here you can email the photos to anyone you would like.

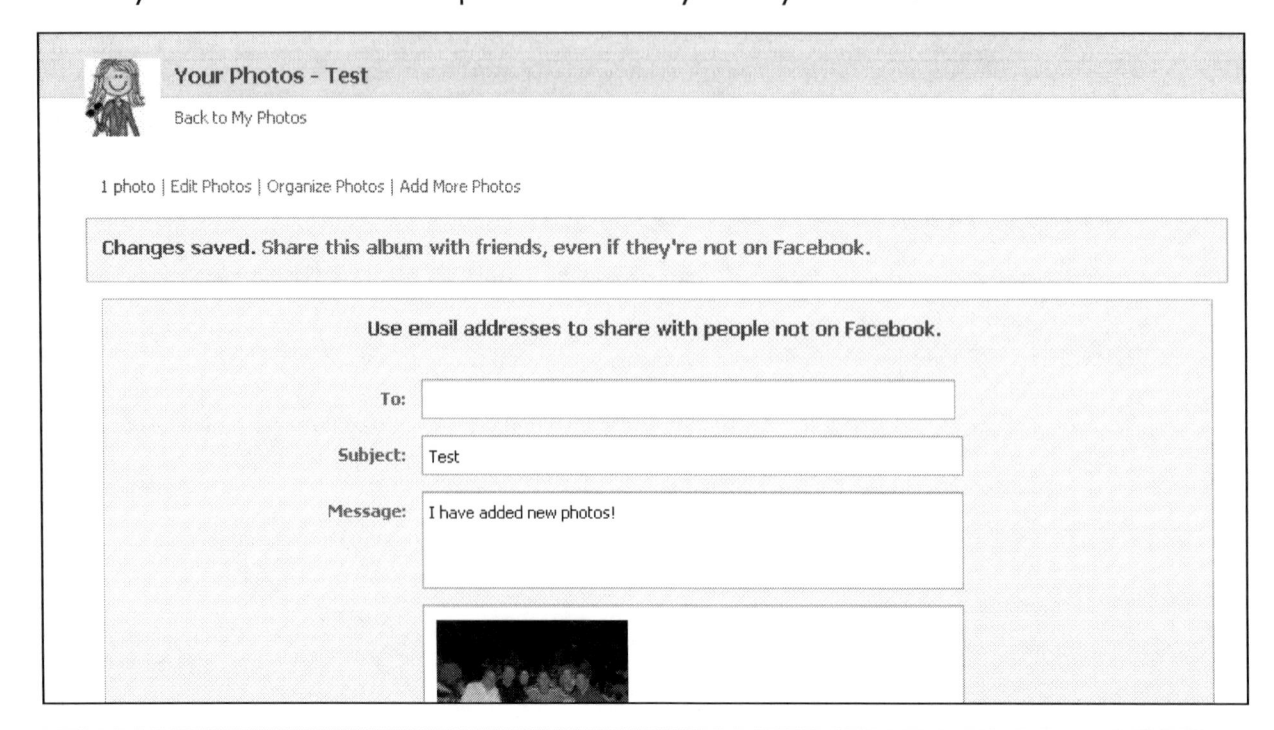

Facebook® Guide for Parents 130

© SupremeSocialMedia.com

Un-tagging Yourself from Photos/Videos:

People can post photos of you without your permission. You can ask the person to remove a photo that you do not think is flattering but they do not have to if they do not want to. One of the ways to mitigate any potential embarrassment is to "un-tag" yourself from photos. This doesn't remove the photo from Facebook, but if someone doesn't know you by your face, it won't identify you to the world.

Click the "Photo" tab on your main profile page. Select the photo on which you would like to remove the tag and click "Remove Tag" under the picture. Once you remove the tag, it is removed from the picture, even if the photo appears in your friend's feed.

Chapter 20: Playing Games on Facebook

Many people like to use Facebook to play games. There are thousands of applications and games you can play on Facebook. You can access games from the left hand side of your home page.

Once you click on "games," you'll go to a page that lists any games you've already installed, games your friends have played recently, and other games and applications your friends use. At the bottom of this page, you'll see a listing of different types of games you can explore including board games, card games, virtual world games, word games etc.

Games

Your Games

Poll (8 friends)
- Played about a week ago

Blessings† (1 friend)
- Played about a month ago

Friends' Recent Activity

On Track Goals (2 friends)
- Jim Bunch played today
- Chris Tunstall played about 2 months ago

Lexulous (1 friend)
- Joanne Sperans played today

FarmVille (42 friends)
- Pat Yuckenberg Gray played today
- Donna Kozik played today
- Tonya Rice played today

FARKLE (11 friends)
- Timothy Johnson played today
- Athena Viratos played about a week ago
- Glory Melucci played about 2 weeks ago

Know-It-All Trivia (2 friends)
- Jennifer Rozenhart Dc played today
- Annette Avery played about a week ago

More | View Your Recent Activity ▸

Friends' Games

- Sorority Life
- Café World
- Birthday Cards

- PathWords
- Super Slot Machines
- Geo Challenge

- FarmVille
- Farm Town
- YoVille

- Café World
- Mafia Wars
- What is your patronus?

See all friends ▸

Featured

Play Tiki Farm
Create the perfect tropical paradise! Grow crops to please the Tiki Spirits. Grass skirt: Optional...
Play Now

Play Happy Aquarium
Rated A+ fun for everyone!
Play Now

Play Happy Pets
Irresistible kittens and puppies are waiting to be adopted by you!
Play Now

Your Facebook Credits Balance
You have 1 Facebook credit. Buy More.

Action & Arcade Games	Board Games	Card Games
MindJolt Games	FARKLE	Texas HoldEm Poker
Bejeweled Blitz	Okey	UNO™
Brain Buddies	Who Has The Bigges...	Poker Rivals
Treasure Madness	Ponzi, Inc.	Poker Palace
Wild Ones	Geo Challenge	麻將－GodGameMJ 神來也麻將
Jungle Jewels	Spot The Difference	德州撲克
Games	Temple of Mahjong 2	World Poker
GooBox - Jeux Grat...	Egg Buddies	Blackjack Madness
Bowling Buddies	Texas Grand Poker	Warstorm
Crazy Planets	Okey Oyna	Bingo World
Action & Arcade Games ▸	Board Games ▸	Card Games ▸

Role Playing Games	Virtual World Games	Word Games
Mafia Wars	FarmVille	Word Challenge
Hero World	Birthday Cards	Three Kingdoms Onl...
Sorority Life	Café World	COLLAPSE!
Castle Age	Happy Aquarium	Typing Maniac

Facebook® Guide for Parents 133

© SupremeSocialMedia.com

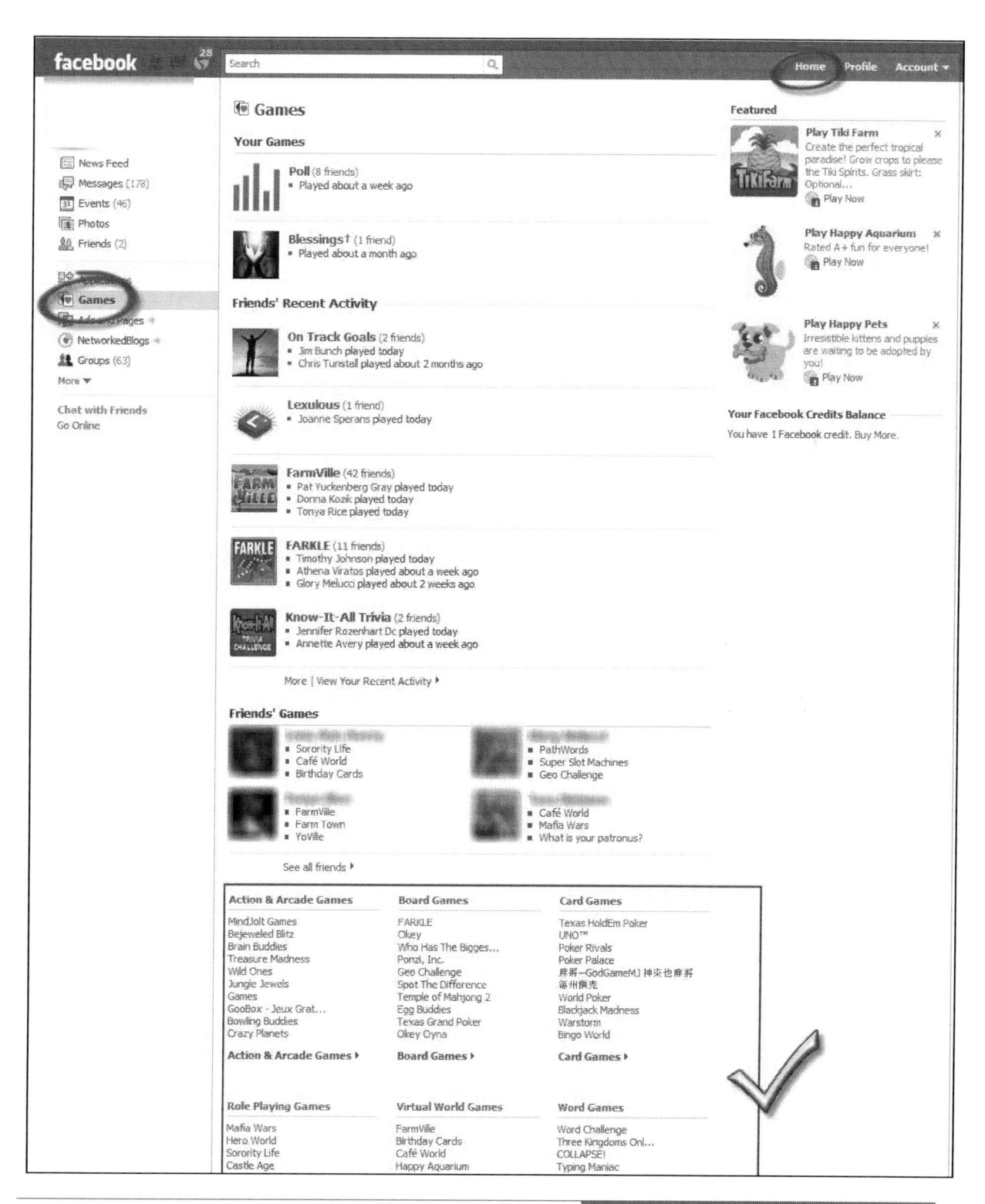

By clicking on any of the categories, you'll be taken to a page where you can choose a game to install. Once you've chosen the application or game, double click on the image and you'll go directly to the application page for that game. Click the "Go to Application" button in blue right under the picture of the game.

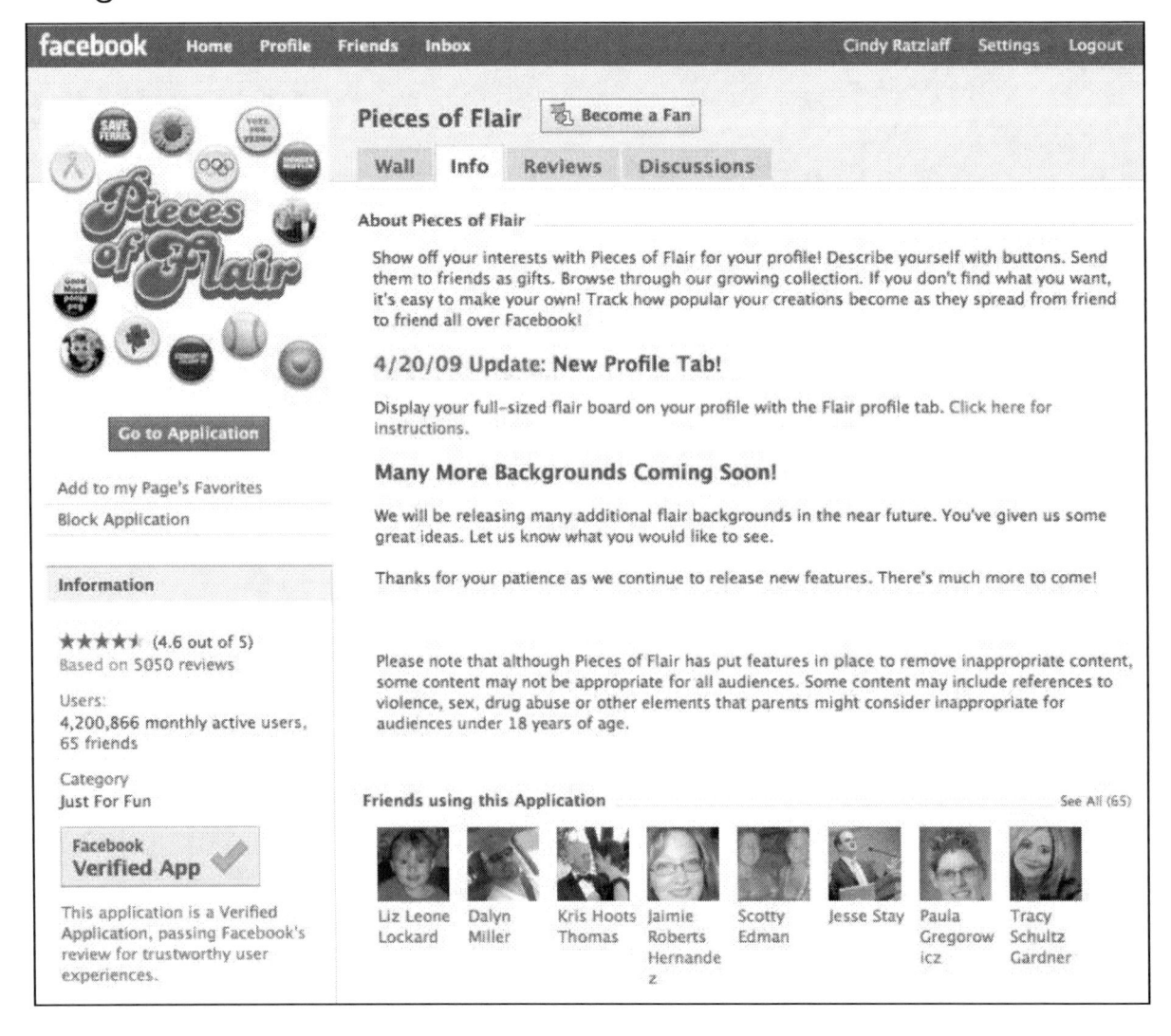

Once you click "Go to application" you'll be taken to a page that asks you to "Allow Access." If you want to install this game, click "Allow."

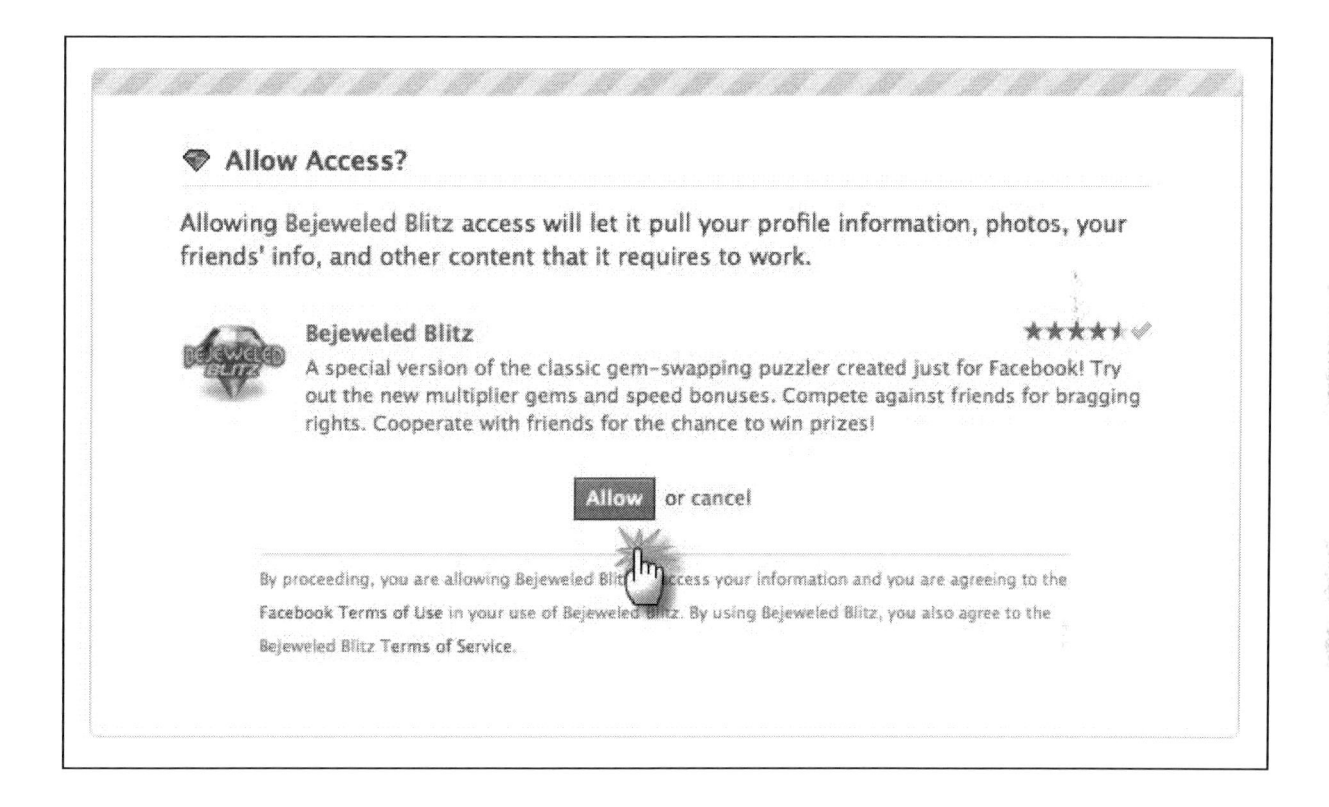

> **Allow Access?**
>
> Allowing Bejeweled Blitz access will let it pull your profile information, photos, your friends' info, and other content that it requires to work.
>
> **Bejeweled Blitz** ★★★★✓
> A special version of the classic gem-swapping puzzler created just for Facebook! Try out the new multiplier gems and speed bonuses. Compete against friends for bragging rights. Cooperate with friends for the chance to win prizes!
>
> **Allow** or cancel
>
> By proceeding, you are allowing Bejeweled Blitz access your information and you are agreeing to the Facebook Terms of Use in your use of Bejeweled Blitz. By using Bejeweled Blitz, you also agree to the Bejeweled Blitz Terms of Service.

Games are a fun way to engage with your child on Facebook, and you can always delete any games you decide you don't like. So have fun exploring the games section of Facebook.

Final Words

We hope that we helped you engage online with your friends, family and colleagues by demystifying some of the social networking concepts.

Be friendly with your kids on Facebook, but never forget being a parent is what they expect of you. It's okay to bring things up that are happening online, because it is just another place where you *all* hang out. Our responsibility, as parents, is to teach our kids how to be kind, polite, respectful, and have good manners in all social situations so they can become respected adults. The online communities are just a bit larger and the messages travel faster, so the importance of learning proper and safe usage right from the beginning is heightened.

We expect that you will have a great experience on Facebook and as you use it on a daily basis, you will become more comfortable and have fun with it.

Let us know how your story of Facebook experience develops. Send us an email to info@supremesocialmedia.com.

Supreme Facebook Contract

We think having a contract between you and your younger teens about their rights and responsibilities when using Facebook can help you set and monitor expectations, start an important conversation between you and your teen and serve as a reminder when rules are ignored. We offer ours as a model and invite you to modify or add to it to represent your individual parenting needs.

While older teens want and need additional autonomy, younger teens need a more omnipresent supervision. So check out our suggested contract for teens under 16 years old. We'd love to hear from you about any additional rules you decide to include. You can post on our Facebook page at http://Facebook.com/SupremeSocialMedia.

© SupremeSocialMedia.com

Family Facebook Users Contract

1. I agree to sit with my parents and go through the privacy settings on my profile and make sure all personal contact information is excluded.
2. I will speak to my parents before accepting someone as a friend.
3. I will ask my parent's permission before uploading any photos to Facebook and then make sure the privacy privileges are set properly.
4. I will take my name off of any Facebook or Search Engine searches
5. I will speak to my parents before downloading any applications on Facebook.
6. My parents will have the username and password to my account and my parents agree not to post anything I deem embarrassing on my wall.
7. I understand that something I post today can be damaging to me in the future so before posting anything I will ask myself "is this something I would want my mother to read?"
8. I will work with my parents to establish online time limits that work for both parties.
9. I will never post anything negative, hurtful or threatening to anyone including family members, teachers or others on Facebook and will tell my parents immediately if I see others doing so.

I understand that any violations of these rules will cause my Facebook privileges to be suspended and may result in my profile begin deleted from Facebook.

Signed _____ Dated_____

Other products by Supreme Social Media

Facebook Guide for Grandparents

http://FBGuideForGrandparents.com

Coming Summer 2010! Great for grandparents who want to keep in touch with their grandkids. Includes module on "Skype" a free service that allows free video and audio calls to stay connected.

Business Products

Beginner's Guide to Social Media

Beginner's Guide to Social Media is an affordable, easy to understand, step-by-step Social Media networking training program that is filled with best practices and strategies for using Facebook and the other top social networks to grow your business.

Don't be a stranger. Visit us on our Fan Page! Feel free to ask us questions about using Facebook and we'll answer with our recommendations.

http://Facebook.com/SupremeSocialMedia

For articles and news about Facebook updates, changes and other interesting items on social media, check out our website

http://SupremeSocial.com

© SupremeSocialMedia.com

Made in the USA
Charleston, SC
04 August 2010